Communications in Computer and Information Science 1569

More information about this series at https://link.springer.com/bookseries/7899

Carlos Brito-Loeza · Anabel Martin-Gonzalez ·
Victor Castañeda-Zeman · Asad Safi (Eds.)

Intelligent Computing Systems

4th International Symposium, ISICS 2022
Santiago, Chile, March 23–25, 2022
Proceedings

Springer

Editors
Carlos Brito-Loeza 🆔
Universidad Autónoma de Yucatán
Merida, Mexico

Anabel Martin-Gonzalez 🆔
Universidad Autónoma de Yucatán
Merida, Mexico

Victor Castañeda-Zeman
Universidad de Chile
Santiago, Chile

Asad Safi 🆔
Higher Colleges of Technology
Abu Dhabi, United Arab Emirates

ISSN 1865-0929 ISSN 1865-0937 (electronic)
Communications in Computer and Information Science
ISBN 978-3-030-98456-4 ISBN 978-3-030-98457-1 (eBook)
https://doi.org/10.1007/978-3-030-98457-1

This Springer imprint is published by the registered company Springer Nature Switzerland AG
The registered company address is: Gewerbestrasse 11, 6330 Cham, Switzerland

Preface

Current technological development, along with faster computer processors, has promoted the generation of an enormous amount of digital data. The capacity of creating and storing information increases the need to implement and improve intelligent systems that automate the analysis and understanding of new datasets to overcome real-world challenges and enhance human life. Capable of perceiving, reasoning, learning, and acting rationally, intelligent systems can make decisions to solve complex and multidisciplinary problems automatically, giving support to the decisions of an expert. Their applications can be numerous and of great variety, including biological sciences, computer vision, robotics, search engines, and data mining, among others. New algorithms and applications are being developed every year, such as deep neural networks, Bayesian networks, kernel machines, feature extraction and dimension reduction, reinforcement learning, self-organizing maps, optimization methods in learning, fuzzy systems, and evolutionary computation, to mention a few.

This book contains written contributions of the Fourth International Symposium on Intelligent Computing Systems (ISICS 2022) held in Santiago de Chile (Chile) during March 23–25, 2022. ISICS is an international conference intended to attract computing professionals to discuss recent developments and trends in software and computing for their research communities. The aim of the conference is to further increase the body of knowledge in this specific area of computer science by providing a forum to exchange ideas and discuss state-of-the-art results. ISICS 2022 was committed to the promotion, preservation, and collaboration of research and practice, focusing on the fields of artificial intelligence, computer vision, and image processing.

For this edition of the conference, we received 30 papers from authors in 13 different countries around the globe. Each submission was evaluated by at least three members of the Program Committee and, based on the reviews, 11 papers were included in the conference program as long oral presentations. In addition to the contributed papers, three keynote speakers were invited to give plenary talks.

We would like to warmly thank all the authors who submitted their work to ISICS 2022. Their contribution to the conference is highly appreciated, and we kindly invite them to continue contributing to future ISICS conferences. We gratefully acknowledge the professional work of the international scientific Program Committee members, and we also greatly appreciate the contribution and participation of our invited speakers, Pascal Fua (Swiss Federal Institute of Technology, Switzerland), Diana Mateus (Centrale Nantes, France), and Hiroaki Kawashima (Kyoto University, Japan). We are very grateful to the Universidad de Chile, Universidad Autónoma de Yucatán, Universidad de

O'Higgins, and Higher Colleges of Technology of the United Arab Emirates for their support in the organization of the ISICS 2022.

March 2022

Carlos Brito-Loeza
Anabel Martin-Gonzalez
Victor Castañeda-Zeman
Asad Safi

Organization

General Chair

Victor Castañeda-Zeman — Universidad de Chile, Chile

Program Committee Chairs

Carlos Brito-Loeza — Universidad Autónoma de Yucatán, México
Anabel Martin-Gonzalez — Universidad Autónoma de Yucatán, México
Asad Safi — Higher Colleges of Technology, UAE

Steering Committee

Bassam Ali — Universidad Autónoma de Yucatán, México
Arturo Espinosa-Romero — Universidad Autónoma de Yucatán, México
Nidiyare Hevia-Montiel — Universidad Nacional Autónoma de México, México
Ricardo Legarda-Saenz — Universidad Autónoma de Yucatán, México
Israel Sánchez-Dominguez — Universidad Nacional Autónoma de México, México
Victor Uc-Cetina — Universidad Autónoma de Yucatán, México

Program Committee

Antonio Aguileta — Universidad Autónoma de Yucatán, México
Noor Badshah — University of Engineering and Technology, Pakistan
Mauricio Cerda — Universidad de Chile, Chile
Luis Curi-Quintal — Universidad Autónoma de Yucatán, México
Yuriria Cortes-Poza — Universidad Nacional Autónoma de México, México
Francisco Hernandez-Lopez — Centro en Investigación en Matemáticas, México
Muhammad Iqbal — Higher Colleges of Technology, UAE
Robinson Jiménez — Universidad Militar Nueva Granada, Colombia
Ricardo Legarda-Saenz — Universidad Autónoma de Yucatán, México
Stacey Levine — Duquesne University, USA
Elena Loli Piccolomini — University of Bologna, Italy
José López-Martinez — Universidad Autónoma de Yucatán, México
Asif Malik — Higher Colleges of Technology, UAE

Salvador Mandujano	Google, USA
Victor Menendez	Universidad Autónoma de Yucatán, México
Iván Meza-Ruiz	Universidad Nacional Autónoma de México, México
Erik Molino	Universidad Nacional Autónoma de México, México
Rafael Morales-Gamboa	Universidad de Guadalajara, México
Raúl Monroy	Instituto Tecnológico de Estudios Superiores de Monterrey, México
Francisco Moo-Mena	Universidad Autónoma de Yucatán, México
Nicolaie Popescu	Higher Colleges of Technology, UAE
Lavdie Rada	Sabanci University, Turkey
Jorge Reyes-Magaña	Universidad Autónoma de Yucatán, México
Eduardo Rodriguez-Martinez	Universidad Autónoma Metropolitana, México
Asad Safi	Higher Colleges of Technology, UAE
Roger Soberanis-Mukul	Technical University of Munich, Germany
Israel Sánchez-Dominguez	Universidad Nacional Autónoma de México, México
Joel Trejo	Centro en Investigación en Matemáticas, México
Victor Uc-Cetina	Universidad Autónoma de Yucatán, México
Rodrigo Verschae	Universidad de Chile, Chile
Jorge Rios-Martinez	Universidad Autónoma de Yucatán, México

Contents

Capable of Classifying the Tuples with Wireless Attacks Detection Using Machine Learning

Tariqul Islam[✉] and Shaikh Muhammad Allayear[✉]

Daffodil International University, Dhaka, Bangladesh
tariqul15-2250@diu.edu.bd, headmct@daffodilvarsity.edu.bd

Abstract. A wireless attack is a malicious action against wireless systems and wireless networks. In the last decade of years, wireless attacks are increasing day by day and it is now a very big problem for modern wireless communication systems. In this paper, the author's used the Aegean Wi-Fi Intrusion Dataset (AWID3). There are two versions of this dataset, one is over 200 million tuples of full data and one is 1.8 million tuples of reduced data. As our dataset has millions of tuples and over 100 columns, it is easy to become overwhelmed because of its size. The authors used the reduced version and predicted if an attack was one of four types using the k-nearest-neighbors classifier. All of the attack types we used had a distribution that highly favored the non-attack class. Our best results were for the attack "arp" type where we attained the best accuracy with recall. The author's primary goal of the paper was to attain the highest accuracy possible when creating a model that is capable of classifying the 4 attack types and detecting and classifying wireless attacks using Machine Learning models on the AWID3 dataset. One of the goals that supported this main objective was determining a way to avoid the curse of dimensionality.

Keywords: Data mining · AWID3 · Cybersecurity · Machine learning · Wireless security

1 Introduction

Wireless attacks have become a very common security issue. Different kinds of attack methods can happen such as "Rogue access points, Jamming or Interference, Evil twin, Wardriving, Bluejacking, Packet sniffing, Near field communication, WEP or WPA attacks, WPS attacks, IV attack, Warchalking".

A rogue access point is an unauthorized access point that can be added to one's wireless network without one's knowledge. Being able to combat this can be done by having network access controls in place or by walking around one's building. The evil twin is a technique used by criminals to gain unauthorized access to a network. With this method, they only need to purchase a wireless access point and then configure it as exactly as the network it's connected to. Doing so allows them to monitor and gain control of all the details of the wireless network. Bluejacking is an illegal practice that enables people to send and receive messages to another device through Bluetooth. This

© Springer Nature Switzerland AG 2022
C. Brito-Loeza et al. (Eds.): ISICS 2022, CCIS 1569, pp. 1–16, 2022.
https://doi.org/10.1007/978-3-030-98457-1_1

is similar to hacking, where the goal is to send an email or a message to another device. Bluesnarfing is a far more dangerous type of attack that involves taking advantage of a vulnerable Bluetooth network to steal sensitive information. This vulnerability can allow an attacker to access a mobile device's contacts and images. War chalking is a method used to determine the location of a wireless access point. An Initialization Vector attack is a type of wireless network attack that can cause modification to the Initialization Vector of a packet. Analyzing the details of a given packet after an attack is performed will allow an attacker to extract valuable information from it. Packet sniffing is a very challenging technique when it comes to wireless networks. In this process, an individual can capture a packet that is sent across a network and see the details of the message that it contains. This feature makes it incredibly easy for an individual to read and hear what's happening in real-time. This technique allows one device to collect data from another device that is in range. An attacker can also collect details about a conversation between two people. An attacker with this kind of information can easily gain access to a computer without its owner's knowledge. He can also use it to prove his identity or authenticate himself. In some cases, a legacy wireless access point can be considered an encryption method that is not suitable for sensitive data. Attacks with the use of WPS passwords are very dangerous and can lead to unauthorized access to a particular network. These types of attacks are usually carried out by criminals who are looking to steal sensitive information. With the help of this tool, an attacker can easily obtain the passwords of wireless networks and gain access to the data and information that is on their network (Fig. 1).

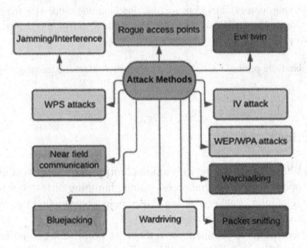

Fig. 1. Different attack methods

2   Related Work

In the paper [1] implementation of AMBA-AXI protocol by using VHDL for SoC (System on a Chip) integration with different components and IPs. But the main challenge in the paper is to verify chip communication properties. They propose a protocol checker such as rule-based AMBA AXI and this contains almost 44 different rules for the check. Bisht et al. [2] develop the first systematic approach for detecting parameter tampering opportunities in web applications and implement this approach in a tool that is called NOTAMPER. This paper presents an approach that combines JavaScript code analysis and black-box vulnerability analysis. It tackles many of the issues traditional methods face in generating and validating inputs. Although it eliminates many of the issues faced by traditional methods, it still requires some effort and compromises. Soleimani et al. [3] research work proposes a black-box method to detect web application vulnerabilities including XSS, CSRF, and information leakage. Takamatsu et al. [4] propose a technique that automatically detects session management vulnerabilities in web applications by simulating real attacks. This method requires the test operator to enter a few details about the web application before testing it. However, it can detect the existence of special characters on the web page. This method can only detect the existence of the special string. Kumar et al. [5] research work propose a detection mechanism of session fixation vulnerability. This paper has limitations like the automated solution architecture of session fixation vulnerability detection has not been defined using any prototype. The model elements are session Id, prepare post request using the valid credential, capture Authenticated session, match authenticated and unauthenticated session. Nadar et al. [6] propose a model that can detect attacks such as cross-site request forgery attacks, broken authentication. Model elements are CSRF: "Request Checker, Packet Tracer, Request Differentiator, Attack Handler, Module, Notify Client, Attack Database Repository". Important result parameters are "True positive, True negative, False positive, False negative, accuracy, Recall, Precision". Dahse and Holz's [7] research paper, they are the first to propose an automated approach to statically analyze second-order data flows through databases, file names, and session variables using string analysis. They propose to detect multi-step and second-order exploitation risks in web applications. They study the issue of second-order sanitization. We discovered 159 previously unknown security issues in the code of our clients. Some of these issues were caused by exploitation techniques such as XSS and remote code execution attacks. Three false negatives were reported in Scarf due to the parser not handling SQL string functions. This vulnerability was discovered in the following list of attacks. Aliero et al. [8] proposed solution is the only solution that performs stored procedure attacks SQL and bypass login authentication even if the returned records are limited restriction is applied. The following steps are needed to trigger SQL injection vulnerability and store procedure vulnerability in web pages. These steps will introduce the necessary vectors and techniques to trigger SQL injection attacks. Ze et al. [9] proposed an efficient Web application vulnerability detection mechanism based on optimized crawler and feature recognition. This research introduces black-box testing ideas and fuzzy testing technology into Web vulnerability detection and realizes a Web vulnerability detection system based on page code analysis and page code analysis modules. Jovanovic et al. [10] proposed flow-sensitive, interprocedural, and context-sensitive data flow analysis. The complexity of the PHP analysis process was due to its untyped nature. Additional steps such as alias analysis and literary analysis lead to more precise and comprehensive results. The proposed system, called Pixy, was developed to address these issues. Marashdih and Zaaba et al. [11]

shows detection of XSS vulnerability, removing the detected vulnerability. But didn't consider an experiment on DOM-based XSS. Medeiros and Neves et al. [12] propose the insights from the behaviors of SATs, they analyze applications written. But the research work is done with only one vulnerability which is SQLi. Lukanta et al. [13] propose to detect session management vulnerabilities, we developed a vulnerability scanning tool extending an existing open-source tool, namely Nikto. But the random token detection mechanism should be revised due to errors in random token detection. Yuan et al. [14] investigate vulnerabilities and analyze the common vulnerabilities in web applications. Anbiya et al. [15] in the paper will present an approach using static analysis with lexical analysis techniques for reducing an expert's knowledge. Lexical analysis is a static analysis technique that transforms source code to other representations, usual tokens for future use. But this research only works with SQL injection, cross-site scripting, and directory traversal. Jeevitha and Bhuvaneswari et al. [16] paper-primarily focus on detecting the malicious node. But some limitations in this paper such as prevention techniques for the malicious nodes are not included in this paper. Pan and Mao et al. [17] propose the notion of DOM-sourced XSS which emphasizes the hierarchical document source and distinguishes it from DOM-based XSS. Mokbal et al. [18] propose extensive real-world data composed of 138,569 unique records to detect XSS attacks that have been constructed comprehensively and uniquely. Kao et al. [19] review different types of SQLi attacks, provide their descriptions, and analyze possible investigative techniques. Moustafa et al. [20] proposed a methodology to automatically capture web data, network traffic data for extracting relevant features. Alswailem et al. [21] feature a combination that comes from the Random Forest technique, as it has high accuracy, is relatively robust and has a good performance. Wang et al. [22] summarize the framework of access control vulnerability detection. Deepa et al. [23] proposed a system called "XiParam"; this prototype is not tested in real-world web applications due to its dependence on the database driver files. Figueiredo et al. [25] developed a learning-based tool that can detect input validation vulnerability using static data flow analysis. But the study did not compare their outcome with another dictation tool. Ibarra-Fiallos et al. [26] design a durable, reliable, and effective protection filter for reducing common web injection attacks. The evolution of web applications, as well as the need to protect them against injection attacks, requires the development of a filter that can safeguard the various parameters of web applications. Choi et al. [27] used static and dynamic analysis approaches, where Static analysis is used to boost up XSS vulnerability detection speed and automatically extracts from a web page and filters out duplicates which saves time.

3 Research Methodology

Here the author's used three different programming languages to assist us: Python, R-Studio, and Microsoft SQL. For Python, the author's used the latest version available at the time of writing Python 3.9.0. In this language, we used the Scikit-Learn, Pandas, and NumPy libraries to help us with our preprocessing steps. Then, in R we used the DMwR library for its SMOTE and K-nearest-neighbors functionality. Finally, we used Server Management Studio to perform queries for Microsoft SQL. We imported the reduced version of our dataset into it to use the SQL server after adding the headers to it. Then reduced AWID3 dataset [28] with only the columns posted on the class web page in Microsoft SQL Server. Lastly, install a streamlet and other dependencies on the system. Ensure both the dataset and the python file are in the same directory. The details about how we were able to achieve this task are authentication discussed in greater detail in our preprocessing and data cleaning section. In the reduced version of the AWID3 dataset, there is a class variable with the values "normal, arp, cafe_latte, amok, deauthentica-tion, authentication_request, beacon, evil_twin, fragmentation, and probe_response". The type normal represents the packets that are not an attack. The other types listed represent an attack. For the author's analysis, chose to use the k-nearest-neighbors clas-sifier algorithm to predict if a packet was of the type: "arp, deauthentication, amok, or authentication_request".

An IP address spoofing attack is another type of attack that uses the address resolution protocol to trick a host into sending traffic to an attacker [29]. A deauthentication attacker uses unprotected deactivation packets. The attacker monitors network traffic to find out which MAC addresses are associated with certain customers. Then, a deauthentication message is sent to the access point on behalf of those particular MAC addresses to force a client of the network. Our third attack type is an authentication request attack. This is a flooding attack in which the attacker tries to exhaust the access point's resources by overflowing their client association table. The last type of attack is an amok attack. Though information on this particular form of cyberattack is limited, we determined that it is another flooding attack on a server, similar to the authentication request. This attack causes the client association table to overflow due to the number of clients that can be maintained there. An entry is inserted into the client association table after an Authentication Request message.

3.1 Processing Method

Build a classifier capable of properly classifying tuples with four specific attack types: Amok, Deauthentication, Authentication Request, ARP. The authors had three major tasks during this work: preprocessing & data cleaning, feature selection, and classification.

3.2 Preprocessing and Data Cleaning

As previously mentioned, we used Python 3.9.0 to perform the majority of our prepro-cessing and data cleaning on our dataset. "The dataset focuses on WPA2 Enterprise, 802.11w, and Wi-Fi 5. It contains multi-layer and modern attacks, including Krack and Kr00k. It is available in pcap format" [30]. AWID3 (Aegean Wi-fi Intrusion) Dataset produced from real Wireless Network logging. This full dataset is shown in Fig. 2 and the reduced training set is shown in Fig. 3 that produced from 1 h of logging. The majority of data is of the "normal" class in either dataset. To do this, we first downloaded the reduced dataset from the dataset's host. Then, by using the read_csv method from the panda's library, we were able to read in a subset of columns that we wanted to work with for our analysis. These 19 desired columns were the following: 2, 5, 45, 62, 64, 65, 68, 71, 74, 75, 88, 91, 92, 105, 106, 110, 116, 120, and 154. After reading in these specific columns, we iterated over a text file containing the attribute names for the columns in our dataset.

If the index of our desired columns existed in that list of attribute names, we added it to a list. Then, we were easily able to set the column headers for our minimized dataset. After we had successfully removed unwanted columns from our larger dataset and given each column a name, we were ready to proceed with the rest of our preprocessing. To start this process, we replaced the question marks in the dataset with a NumPy NaN value. The authors performed this operation to enable us to use other methods provided in the panda library to remove missing values from our data set. After replacing these values, we iterated over the columns in our dataset and removed a column if over 60% of its values were NaN (Not A Number). If a large majority of a column in the dataset was NaN, then it was not going to be useful for our later analysis. By performing this step, we removed 7 columns from our already minimized dataset. Then we removed columns that had zero or one unique value. A column had zero unique values if there were no values provided, but was not filled in with a NaN value. In contrast, a column would have one unique value if it had the same value for every tuple. This target data would not contribute to our future analysis in both of these situations because there was nothing to help distinguish a tuple with a normal class value or one of our four attack types. As a final step in preprocessing and cleaning our dataset, we removed the rows with a target of at least one NaN value left. By doing this, we removed 1972 rows from the dataset. In hindsight, more caution should have been exercised when doing this as these tuples with a NaN value could have helped us further identify anomalies in the dataset. Last, after performing all these steps, we exported the reduced dataset as a CSV file for later use in our analysis. All of the code for performing the operations described in this section are shown in data_preprocessing_cleaning.py.

AWID-ATK-F-Trn		AWID-ATK-R-Trn	
12416	amok	31180	amok
1529284	arp	64609	arp
93011	authentication_request	3500	authentication_request
170826	beacon	1799	beacon
1860780	cafe_latte	45889	cafe_latte
817954	deauthentication	10447	deauthentication
23598	evil_twin	2633	evil_twin
1889	fragmentation	770	fragmentation
157749037	normal	1633198	normal
117252	probe_response	1558	probe_response

Fig. 2. AWID3 Full dataset to reduced training dataset (~1.8 Million Rows x 155 Columns)

Dropped columns not listed on the course webpage. Replaced '?' with NaN values, then dropped columns with over 60% NaN values and removed 7 columns. Drop the rows with at least one NaN value in it – 2000 rows. Output the relatively clean data to anew file. Perform min-max normalization on attributes used for classification (range 0–1).

1	0.0	0.000000e+00	0.00310559	normal
2	0.0	6.929365e-02	0.00310559	normal
3	0.0	4.656501e-03	0.00310559	normal
4	0.0	1.579527e-01	0.00310559	normal
5	1.0	1.184824e-03	0.64285714	normal
6	0.5	1.427499e-05	0.00310559	normal
7	0.0	4.765562e-02	0.00310559	normal
8	0.5	4.054096e-04	0.00310559	normal
9	0.0	8.013122e-02	0.00310559	normal
10	0.0	5.141851e-03	0.00310559	normal
11	0.0	3.567034e-02	0.00310559	normal
12	1.0	6.566494e-05	0.64285714	normal
13	0.5	1.084899e-04	0.00310559	normal
14	0.0	1.219912e-01	0.00310559	normal
15	0.0	7.223715e-02	0.00310559	normal
16	1.0	1.800932e-02	0.64285714	normal
17	0.5	1.427499e-05	0.00310559	normal
18	1.0	6.480844e-03	0.64285714	normal

Fig. 3. Normalization output

3.3 Feature Selection

To select which columns we would use with the classifier we first removed all columns except the columns listed on the course webpage. We then went through them by hand looking for attacks that had null values (? 's in our case) and non-null values for the normal type or vise-versa. None were found so we went on to the next step where we removed many null valued columns and rows (see the preprocessing/data cleaning section). Next, we used the following SQL query: Select Count (Distinct(<COLUMN_NAME>)) from <AWID_DATABASE> where class = '<CLASSTYPE>' where <CLASSTYPE> equaled the normal and all attack classes we used and <COLUMN_NAME> was varied to equal the remaining columns in our data. Before deciding that a column wasn't going to be removed we looked at the data further to make sure that even if all classes had the same number of distinct values that they weren't different distinct values for the attack and the normal type. Below are the results of these queries and our analysis of them. We didn't choose the radiotap_flags_shortgi column because it had no variation. We chose the wlan_fc_type column because after looking at it further it showed that the normal class type varied highly among 3 values while the attack types all had the same values and this frame_time_delta_displayed variable because upon looking further into it we saw that for the attack types all the tuples had very close values while the normal type was more spread out. We didn't choose the wlan_fc_version, wlan_fcs_good, frame_offset_shift, frame_offset_shift and radiotap_rxflags_badplcp variable because of the lack of variation. And also the wlan_duration variable because there is a lot of variation for type normal and barely any for those whose class value is one of the four attack types.

After much debate, we decided to not use this variable (wlan_ra) even though it has the variation we are looking for because it is nominal and not ordinal and the rest of our variables are continuous. Since SMOTE only works for continuous variables we felt it would be best not to use it otherwise we would probably have to one-hot-encode all of our data and use a different classifier than K-Nearest-Neighbors and not use SMOTE. We didn't choose this attribute (wlan_fc_moredata) because even though it has the variation we were looking for, 99.99% of the normal tuples had the same value as the attack types making it useless. The authors attempted PCA but ran out of memory even on CSU's Big Data Servers. We examined distinct values in the remaining columns and chose those with more distinct values for the normal class value than the attack class values using a little SQL magic. Then, chose the following 3 columns for our analysis and Isolated the attack types. Separate files to handle each attack type are shown in Fig. 4.

```
KNN-CONTINUOUS-AMOK.R
KNN-CONTINUOUS-ARP.R
KNN-CONTINUOUS-AUTHENTICATION_REQUEST.R
KNN-CONTINUOUS-DEAUTHENTICATION.R
```

Fig. 4. Handle each attack

Partitioned dataset into 66.6% training data and 33.3% test data. Performed SMOTE on training data to create synthetic tuples of attack types. K-Nearest Neighbor classifier to train the model for each specific attack type. Made predictions using the model on the test dataset. Parameter Selection/Interpretation Recall - "completeness – what % of positive tuples did the classifier label as positive?" Recall = TP/TP + FN and Precision - "exactness – what % of tuples that the classifier labeled as positive are positive" that means Precision = TP/TP + FP. Recall and precision are inversely related measures, meaning as precision increases, recall decreases. Accuracy and recall are inversely related in our case (for a majority of our data).

3.4   Classification

Our classification code is written in R. We chose this because it was already known by the group member that wrote the classification code. To perform classification we decided early that we would use SMOTE to create synthetic minority class tuples because the dataset is highly biased towards the normal class. We decided on using the K-nearest-neighbor classification algorithm later. We chose the k-nearest-neighbor algorithm because it works well with continuous data and every variable we used to classify was continuous. To perform the classification we first min-max normalized all of our target attributes to [0, 1]. Next, we removed all classes except the normal and the attack class that we were currently predicting. Then, we randomly divided the normalized dataset into 66.6% training and 33.3% test datasets. Next, we fed the training data into the function SMOTE() in R studio. Then, we fed the oversampled resulting training dataset from SMOTE and the test dataset into the function kNN() in R. From the kNN() function we received a vector containing a 0 or 1 depending upon if the attack class was predicted. We used different operands for the SMOTE() and kNN() functions depending upon if we wanted higher recall or higher accuracy. We attempted cross-validation but due to an error we received ("too many ties"), we were not able to complete it.

4   Result and Discussion

We performed multiple tests on each attack type and recorded our top two, except for ARP. Our results for ARP were extremely good, which made it very challenging to further improve them. We either ran into errors or achieved similar results each time we attempted to modify the parameters. By tuning the parameters for SMOTE and the KNN classifier we were able to improve our accuracy and precision for each of the other attacks, but at the cost of the recall. Several tables displaying the results and parameters used for each of the four attacks can be seen below. We are quite certain the results for ARP were significantly better than the other three attacks because some of the variables for ARP had mutually exclusive values, while the same variables for the other attack type shared values with the normal type. For example, for ARP the fc_type variable was always 0 and the wlan_duration variable for ARP was always the same while that was not the case for the other attacks. Performed multiple tests for each attack. ARP (Test 1) KNN Parameters - Smote.k = 3, KNN.k = 5, smote.perc.over = 150, smote.perc.under = 90 Confusion Matrix - N = 576,582 (Tables 1, 2 and 3).

Table 1. ARP (Address Resolution Protocol) Test 1

	Predicted: NO	Predicted: YES	Total
Actual: NO	552,958	1,731	554,689
Actual: YES	4	21,889	21,893
Total	552,962	23,620	

Table 2. ARP (Test 1) - Anomaly Detection Metrics

False positives	1,731
True positives	21,889
True negatives	552,958
False negatives	4

Only one set of results with ARP. Difficult to improve on already extremely good results for ARP. Amok (Test 1) KNN Parameters - Smote.k = 3, knn.k = 5, smote.perc.over = 150, smote.perc.under = 90. Amok (Test 1) - Confusion Matrix - N = 565,216 (Tables 4, 5 and 6).

Amok (Test 2) KNN Parameters- smote.k = 1, knn.k = 1, smote.perc.over = 120, smote.perc.under = 200. Amok (Test 2) - Confusion Matrix - N = 565,216 (Tables 7, 8 and 9).

Table 3. ARP (Test 1) - Anomaly Detection Metrics (Contd.)

Accuracy	99.6990%
Error rate	0.3009%
Sensitivity	92.6714%
Specificity	99.9992%
Precision	92.6714%
Recall	99.9817%

Table 4. Amok (Test 1)

	Predicted: NO	Predicted: YES	Total
Actual: NO	511,451	42,928	554,379
Actual: YES	562	10,275	10,837
Total	512,013	53,203	

Table 5. Amok (Test 1) - Anomaly Detection Metrics

False positives	42,928
True positives	10,275
True negatives	511,451
False negatives	562

Table 6. Amok (Test 1) - Anomaly Detection Metrics (Contd.)

Accuracy	92.3056%
Error rate	7.6944%
Sensitivity	19.3128%
Specificity	99.8902%
Precision	19.3128%
Recall	94.8140%

Table 7. Amok (Test 2)

	Predicted: NO	Predicted: YES	Total
Actual: NO	529,906	24,473	554,379
Actual: YES	1099	9,738	10,837
Total	531,005	34,211	

Table 8. Amok (Test 2) - Anomaly Detection Metrics

False positives	24,473
True positives	9,738
True negatives	529,906
False negatives	1099

Table 9. Amok (Test 2) - Anomaly Detection Metrics (Contd.)

Accuracy	95.4757%
Error rate	4.5242%
Sensitivity	2.8464%
Specificity	99.7930%
Precision	28.4645%
Recall	89.8588%

Deauthentication (Test 1) KNN Parameters - Smote.k = 3, knn.k = 5, smote.perc.over = 150, smote.perc.under = 90. Deauthentication (Test 1) - Confusion Matrix - N = 558,167 (Tables 10, 11 and 12).

Table 10. Deauthentication (Test 1)

	Predicted: NO	Predicted: YES	Total
Actual: NO	512,542	42,022	554,564
Actual: YES	95	3,508	3,603
Total	512,637	45,530	

Table 11. Deauthentication (Test 1) - Anomaly Detection Metrics

False positives	42,022
True positives	3,508
True negatives	512,542
False negatives	95

Deauthentication (Test 2) KNN Parameters - smote.k = 1, knn.k = 1, smote.perc.over = 90, smote.perc.under = 400. Deauthentication (Test 2) - Confusion Matrix - N = 558,167 (Tables 13, 14 and 15).

Table 12. Deauthentication (Test 1) - Anomaly Detection Metrics (Contd.)

Accuracy	92.4544%
Error rate	7.5455%
Sensitivity	7.7048%
Specificity	99.9814%
Precision	7.7048%
Recall	97.3633%

Table 13. Deauthentication (Test 2)

	Predicted: NO	Predicted: YES	Total
Actual: NO	527,780	26,784	554,564
Actual: YES	379	3,224	3,603
Total	528,159	30,008	

Table 14. Deauthentication (Test 2) - Anomaly Detection Metrics

False positives	26,784
True positives	3,224
True negatives	527,780
False negatives	379

Table 15. Deauthentication (Test 2) - Anomaly Detection Metrics (Contd.)

Accuracy	95.1335%
Error rate	4.8664%
Sensitivity	10.7438%
Specificity	99.9282%
Precision	10.7438%
Recall	89.4809%

Authentication Request (Test 1) KNN Parameters - Smote.k = 3, knn.k = 5, smote.perc.over = 150, smote.perc.under = 90. Authentication Request (Test 1) - Anomaly Detection Metrics - N = 555,805 (Tables 16, 17 and 18).

Table 16. Authentication request (Test 1)

	Predicted: NO	Predicted: YES	Total
Actual: NO	513,668	40,945	554,613
Actual: YES	31	1,161	1,192
Total	513,699	42,106	

Table 17. Authentication request (Test 1) - Anomaly Detection Metrics

False positives	40,945
True positives	1,161
True negatives	513,668
False negatives	31

Table 18. Authentication request (Test 1) - Anomaly Detection Metrics (Contd.)

Accuracy	92.6276%
Error rate	7.3723%
Sensitivity	2.7573%
Specificity	99.9939%
Precision	2.7573%
Recall	97.3993%

Table 19. Authentication request (Test 2)

	Predicted: NO	Predicted: YES	Total
Actual: NO	540,840	13,773	554,613
Actual: YES	152	1,040	1,192
Total	540,992	14,813	

Authentication Request (Test 2) KNN Parameters-Smote.k = 1, knn.k = 1, smote.perc.over = 100, smote.perc.under = 300. Authentication Request (Test 2) - Anomaly Detection Metrics - N = 555,805 (Tables 19, 20 and 21).

Table 20. Authentication request (Test 2) - Anomaly Detection Metrics

False positives	13,773
True positives	1,040
True negatives	540,840
False negatives	152

Table 21. Authentication request (Test 2) - Anomaly Detection Metrics (Contd.)

Accuracy	97.4946%
Error rate	2.5053%
Sensitivity	7.0208%
Specificity	99.9719%
Precision	7.0208%
Recall	87.2483%

5   Conclusion and Future Work

This paper used the k-nearest-neighbor classifier to predict if data from the AWID dataset was normal or an attack. Our results were mixed with either high accuracy and high recall, high accuracy, and lower recall, or high recall and lower accuracy. Most of our time was spent on deciding how to pre-process the data, deciding which features to use with the classifier, and deciding which classifier and oversampling method to use. We learned a lot from the paper but if we could do it again we would select more features to classify with. In a future version, we would like to try using a classifier with the 3 variables we used plus the wlan_ra (MAC address) variable that we didn't use to see how it affects accuracy and recall for the 3 attacks that had lackluster results. To do this we would have to use plain oversampling instead of SMOTE, one-hot-encoding, and probably use a different classifier such as neural network which is compatible with one-hot encoding. Additionally, we would like to test a more generalized model that simply determines if an attack occurred. By generalizing the model, the performance would most likely be improved.

References

1. Ranga, A., Venkatesh, L.H., Venkanna, V.: Design and implementation of AMBA-AXI protocol using VHDL for Soc integration. Int. J. Eng. Res. Appl. (IJERA) **2**, 1102–1106 (2012)
2. Bisht, P.: Notamper: automatic BlackBox detection of parameter tampering opportunities in web applications. In: Proceedings of the 17th ACM Conference on Computer and Communications Security (2010)

3. Soleimani, H., Hadavi, M.A., Bagherdaei, A.: WAVE: black-box detection of XSS, CSRF and information leakage vulnerabilities. In: 2017 14th International ISC (Iranian Society of Cryptology) Conference on Information Security and Cryptology (ISCISC). IEEE (2017)
4. Takamatsu, Y., Kosuga, Y., Kono, K.: Automated detection of session management vulnerabilities in web applications. In: 2012 Tenth Annual International Conference on Privacy, Security, and Trust. IEEE (2012)
5. Kumar, R., Goel, A.K.: Automated session fixation vulnerability detection in web applications using the set-cookie HTTP response header in cookies. In: Proceedings of the 7th International Conference on Security of Information and Networks (2014)
6. Nadar, V.M., Chatterjee, M., Jacob, L.: A defensive approach for CSRF and broken authentication and session management attack. In: Perez, G., Tiwari, S., Trivedi, M., Mishra, K. (eds.) Ambient Communications and Computer Systems, pp. 577–588. Springer, Singapore (2018).https://doi.org/10.1007/978-981-10-7386-1_49
7. Dahse, J., Holz, T.: Static detection of second-order vulnerabilities in web applications. In: 23rd {USENIX} Security Symposium ({USENIX} Security 14) (2014)
8. Aliero, M.S., et al.: Detection of structure query language injection vulnerability in a with target web-driven database application. Concurr. Comput.: Pract. Exp. e5936 (2020)
9. Ze, W.: Design and implementation of core modules of WEB application vulnerability detection model. In: 2019 11th International Conference on Measuring Technology and Mechatronics Automation (ICMTMA). IEEE (2019)
10. Jovanovic, N., Kruegel, C., Kirda, E.: Pixy: a static analysis tool for detecting web application vulnerabilities. In: 2006 IEEE Symposium on Security and Privacy (S&P'06). IEEE (2006)
11. Marashdih, A.W., Zaaba, Z.F.: Detection and removing cross-site scripting vulnerability in PHP web application. In: 2017 International Conference on Promising Electronic Technologies (ICPET). IEEE (2017)
12. Medeiros, I., Neves, N.: Effect of coding styles in detection of web application vulnerabilities. In: 2020 16th European Dependable Computing Conference (EDCC). IEEE (2020)
13. Lukanta, R., Asnar, Y., Imam Kistijantoro, A.: A vulnerability scanning tool for session management vulnerabilities. In: 2014 International Conference on Data and Software Engineering (ICODSE). IEEE (2014)
14. Yuan, H., et al.: Research and implementation of security vulnerability detection in application system of WEB static source code analysis based on JAVA. In: Xu, Z., Choo, K.K., Dehghantanha, A., Parizi, R., Hammoudeh, M. (eds.) The International Conference on Cyber Security Intelligence and Analytics, 444–452. Springer, Cham (2019). https://doi.org/10.1007/978-3-030-15235-2_66
15. Anbiya, D.R., Purwarianti, A., Asnar, Y.: Vulnerability detection in PHP web application using lexical analysis approach with machine learning. In: 2018 5th International Conference on Data and Software Engineering (ICoDSE). IEEE (2018)
16. Jeevitha, R., Sudha Bhuvaneswari, N.: Malicious node detection in VANET session hijacking attack. In: 2019 IEEE International Conference on Electrical, Computer and Communication Technologies (ICECCT). IEEE (2019)
17. Pan, J., Mao, X.: Detecting DOM-sourced cross-site scripting in browser extensions. In: 2017 IEEE International Conference on Software Maintenance and Evolution (ICSME). IEEE (2017)
18. Mokbal, F.M.M., et al.: MLPXSS: an integrated XSS-based attack detection scheme in web applications using multilayer perceptron technique. IEEE Access 7, 100567–100580 (2019)
19. Kao, D.-Y., Lai, C.-J., Su, C.-W.: A framework for SQL injection investigations: detection, investigation, and forensics. In: 2018 IEEE International Conference on Systems, Man, and Cybernetics (SMC). IEEE (2018)

20. Moustafa, N., Misra, G., Slay, J.: Generalized outlier Gaussian mixture technique based on automated association features for simulating and detecting web application attacks. IEEE Trans. Sustain. Comput. (2018)
21. Alswailem, A., et al.: Detecting phishing websites using machine learning. In: 2019 2nd International Conference on Computer Applications & Information Security (ICCAIS). IEEE (2019)
22. Wang, Q., et al.: Access control vulnerabilities detection for web application components. In: 2020 IEEE 6th International Conference on Big Data Security on Cloud (BigDataSecurity), IEEE International Conference on High Performance and Smart Computing, (HPSC), and IEEE International Conference on Intelligent Data and Security (IDS). IEEE (2020)
23. Deepa, G., et al.: Black-box detection of XQuery injection and parameter tampering vulnerabilities in web applications. Int. J. Inf. Secur. 17(1), 105–120 (2018)
24. Kurniawan, A., et al.: Static taint analysis traversal with object-oriented component for web file injection vulnerability pattern detection. Procedia Comput. Sci. 135, 596–605 (2018)
25. Figueiredo, A., Lide, T., Correia, M.: Multi-language web vulnerability detection. In: 2020 IEEE International Symposium on Software Reliability Engineering Workshops (ISSREW). IEEE (2020)
26. Ibarra-Fiallos, S., et al.: Effective filter for common injection attacks in online web applications. IEEE Access 9, 10378–10391 (2021)
27. Choi, H., et al.: HXD: Hybrid XSS detection by using a headless browser. In: 2017 4th International Conference on Computer Applications and Information Processing Technology (CAIPT). IEEE (2017)
28. Chatzoglou, E., Kambourakis, G., Kolias, C.: Empirical evaluation of attacks against IEEE 802.11 enterprise networks: the AWID3 dataset. IEEE Access 9, 34188–34205 (2021)
29. Address resolution protocol From - Wikipedia, the free encyclopedia. Accessed 27 June 2021. https://en.wikipedia.org/wiki/Address_Resolution_Protocol
30. University of the Aegean - AWID3 datasets including Krack and Kr00k. It is available in pcap format. Accessed 1 July 2021. https://icsdweb.aegean.gr/awid/download-dataset

Fault Diagnosis of Combustion Engines in MTU 16VS4000-G81 Generator Sets Using Fuzzy Logic: An Approach to Normalize Specific Fuel Consumption

J. C. Fernández[1]([⊠]) [ID], L. B. Corrales[2] [ID], I. F. Benítez[3] [ID], and J. R. Núñez[4] [ID]

[1] Department of Operations, Generating Sets and Electric Services,
85100 Bayamo, Granma, Cuba
jcfernandez@grm.geysel.une.cu

[2] Faculty of Electromechanics, Department of Electrical Engineering, University of Camagüey,
70100 Camagüey, Cuba
luis.corrales@reduc.edu.cu

[3] Faculty of Electrical Engineering, Department of Automatic Control Engineering,
University of Oriente, 90500 Santiago of Cuba, Cuba
ibenitez@uo.edu.cu

[4] Faculty of Engineering, Department of Engineering,
University of the Costa, 080002 Barranquilla, Colombia
jnunez22@cuc.edu.co

Abstract. The availability of combustion engines used in generating sets is essential for the continuity of electrical service in industrial and service processes. There are different diagnostic methods that use artificial intelligence techniques to detect flaws in combustion engines such as ANN, SVM, etc. Although these methods have good results, they are so complicated that they are difficult to implement in practice. Another drawback is that they find restrictions in the detection of multiple faults and in providing a diagnosis that serves as the basis for improving important aspects such as maintenance management and fuel efficiency. This work presents a method of diagnosing faults in the MTU-16V-S4000-G81 internal combustion engines using fuzzy logic tools. The proposal is based on historical data of the process and allows the detection of the incipient deviation of the main parameters that alter the fuel consumption index. It guarantees 96.9% multiple fault detection and offers a fuzzy method that suggests maintenance actions to restore specific fuel consumption to normal immediately, facilitating efficient maintenance management.

Keywords: Combustion engines · Fault diagnosis · Fuzzy logic · Fuel consumption

1 Introduction

The advance in fault diagnosis methods (FDI) sensitive to incipient failures is considered a problem of great importance for the industry where the availability, safety and

© Springer Nature Switzerland AG 2022
C. Brito-Loeza et al. (Eds.): ISICS 2022, CCIS 1569, pp. 17–29, 2022.
https://doi.org/10.1007/978-3-030-98457-1_2

continuity of the electrical service are fundamental aspects. For this reason, the need to detect small failures that reduce repair costs and implement intelligent techniques that affect operation and maintenance grows every day. FDIs that use historical data are essential for today's industries as they are an advantage in very complex systems, where the relationships between variables are non-linear and where it is very difficult to determine a model efficiently.

In this context, a large number of investigations have been developed, based on the history of the process, that use fuzzy logic techniques in internal combustion engines (MCI, by its acronym in spanish) to detect faults with very good results [1–4]. When reviewing the scientific and technical literature with a focus on diagnostic methods in combustion engines, it was found that the two most widely used fault classification tools today are Artificial Neural Networks (ANN) and Vector Support Machines (SVM). In [5–8] and in [9, 10] the classifying methods that have the best generalization results have been used using ANN and SVM respectively. However, in [11–13] the authors have combined intelligent techniques to establish hybrid methods that allow higher precision in the detection of failures.

Making an evaluation of the most used techniques, an increase in fuzzy logic in this field of scientific research for internal failures in combustion engines is appreciated [14]. The study considered its acceptance and contribution to establish the limit conditions in the main operating variables. This technique offers great advantages related to the treatment of imprecise data, with ambiguity and uncertainties that are present in the modeling of non-linear processes, such as the behavior of gases, oil and temperature in the process of generating.

In previous works, an important contribution was demonstrated in the identification of simple failures based on the monitoring of possible variables of interest that reach or exceed a certain threshold. Although good results are obtained, these methods find restrictions in detecting multiple failures and in improving important aspects such as maintenance and efficiency. This drawback reduces its diagnostic capacity, which justifies the need to continue improving, through intelligent techniques, fault diagnosis systems in this field of scientific research.

Taking into account the above, the objective of this work is to design a fault diagnosis method in the combustion engines of MTU 16V-S4000-G81 electrogen groups (EG). The proposal is based on historical data and presents an approach to normalize specific fuel consumption using fuzzy logic tools. This method allows the identification of multiple faults and the detection of the incipient deviation of the fuel consumption index. It also offers a method that suggests actions to restore the specific fuel consumption (SFC) to the regulated value, which facilitates efficient maintenance management.

2 Materials and Methods

The current electricity demand in the world based on the use of diesel fuel is 27004.7TWh. Of this, in the countries of Asia and the Pacific, energy expenditure is 46.9%, in North America it is 20.1%, in Europe it is 14.8%, in South and Central America it is 4.9% and in the rest it is 13.8% [15]. In Cuba, 95% of the energy matrix is based on fossil fuels and in the electricity generation process the use of diesel generators is essential to cover the peaks in demand of the National Electro-energy System (SEN, by its acronym in spanish).

All the diesel technology that is maintained and administered by the company of Generating Sets and Electric Services (GEYSEL, by its acronym in spanish) in Cuba comprises 149 power plants distributed of two types: 54 of the battery and 95 of the station or isolated. Of these, 55.3% correspond to generators with combustion engines of the MTU 16V-S4000-G81 type, 17.6% to MTU 16V-S4000-G83 groups, while 27.1% correspond to other technologies.

This MTU technology in the country has more than 1200 MW installed and uses the highest international cost fuel for electricity generation [16]. That is why the development of intelligent diagnostic methods to SFC constitutes one of the greatest challenges today. For this reason, it was decided to choose the MTU-16V-S4000-G81 engines as the object for the design of the proposed diagnostic method.

2.1 An Overview of the MTU 16V S4000 G-81 Combustion Engine

The present study was developed in 40 MTU combustion engines belonging to three power plants managed by the GEYSEL in the province of Granma, Cuba. This entity is responsible for the maintenance and diagnosis of diesel generators that synchronize the SEN. These MTU-16V-S4000-G81 engines constitute a fundamental element within the generation system of each power plant. For this reason, the development of fault diagnosis methods in generator sets is based on identifying the changes that prevent the generator and/or the MCI from working normally, putting them at risk of deterioration, being the symptoms of power failures. the latter are the ones that have the greatest impact on the efficiency [17].

These MTU G81 groups have a weight of with 16.4 tons. The designation of the model 16V-S4000 is due to the fact that the engine has 16 cylinders that work in V. Their diameters are 19 cm and the stroke of the piston ranges from 4.06 to 4.69 L. They are capable of working at a temperature ranging from −54 °C (219 K) to 80 °C (353 K). In Cuba, these engines work at an average temperature of 32 °C (305 K) and at an average humidity of 80%. Its power output is 1900 kW and its rated speed is 1800 rpm.

The direction of engine rotation is clockwise when viewed from the flywheel side. Its distribution system is composed of a camshaft, a free gear, two high and low temperature water pumps coupled to the crankshaft and finally a lubrication pump. The hot air due to the operation of the motor is forced out into the atmosphere by 3 induced draft electric fans with a capacity of 10,200 m^3/h of air flow each.

The management system on the MTU-16V4000-G81 consists of an engine control unit (ECU) that is integrated into a cast iron housing with a screw-on cover and has integrated software that controls the starting sequence. The pre-setting of the rotational speed is compared by the nominal speed regulator with the real rotational speed of the motor. In case of differences, it adapts its output signal (nominal amount of fuel injection) according to the difference.

Figure 1 shows the motor regulation circuit. The characteristic of the represented controller has the function of guaranteeing a quick reaction to changes and an exact adjustment of the rotational speed with the lowest with the lowest fuel consumption.

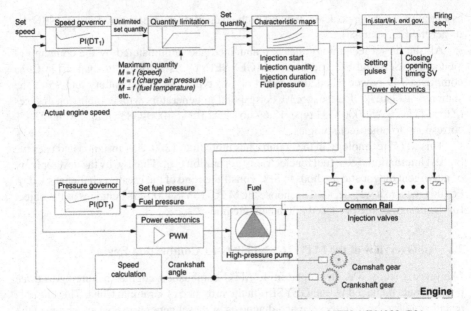

Fig. 1. Regulation block diagram of the combustion engine MTU-16V4000-G81.

Although this regulation scheme guarantees high efficiency in fuel consumption in the MTU-16V4000-G81, it is necessary to develop intelligent techniques that guarantee the identification of multiple faults and the detection of the incipient deviation of the parameters that directly affect the fuel consumption. Given this need, the design proposal includes a fuzzy logic method for fault detection that suggests actions to restore the (SFC) to the standard value, which facilitates efficient maintenance management.

2.2 Description of the Design Proposal

It should be noted that one of the fundamental aspects in the design of fault diagnosis methods that use artificial intelligence tools is the treatment of the signals from the process. Ultimately, it is a matter of extracting and encoding, from the signals, that useful information about the faults that must be detected or diagnosed. If the objective is to evaluate these signals to decide on the status of the process, mechanisms must be established to deal with the various problems that may affect them, such as imprecision, uncertainty, absence or excessive amount of information [18].

Making an analysis of the different techniques developed in recent years in the diagnosis of faults, an increase in the use of fuzzy logic based on historical data in combustion engines with very good precision results can be seen [1–4]. These methods have been considered a topic of great importance for the development of diagnostic systems sensitive to small-magnitude failures in today's industries, especially when there is no precise information on the process, or models that incorporate the failures, as is the case of an MTU-16V4000-G81 engine.

In order to comply with the strict legislation on gas emissions, guarantee correct operation and improve the efficiency of the engine, the injectors must be monitored [19].

From the literature review, it was found that most model-based diagnostic methods use process models or signals are designed based on state observers, parameter estimation, process signal analysis models.

Although these works reviewed good results, they constitute difficult methods to implement in practice due to the complexity of the non-linear systems present in processes such as combustion in the MTU-16V4000-G81 where efficiency in the use of fuel is essential. Bearing in mind the above, in [20] the authors designed a model that allowed to rank the mechanical systems that make up internal combustion engines. This model demonstrated that the most critical systems were the fuel injection, intake and exhaust gas and engine cooling systems.

From the analysis of the generation process, the historical records of the supervision, control and data acquisition (SCADA) system, the main incidents in the interruptions in the combustion engines were collected. From it, it was determined that the most frequent faults that affect the analyzed engines are located in the governor of the high pressure pump, fuel heat exchanger, injection and charge air supply system. Therefore, it was decided to diagnose the following faults: high pressure pump failure (F1), coolant leaking (F2), faulty injector (F3), fuel filter clogging (F4) and multiple faults (F5).

The diagnostic proposal conceptualizes as a mixture of faults or multiple faults (Fm) all the cases in which deviations of two or more simple faults of the type F1, F2, F3 and F4 appear simultaneously.

In the literature consulted, it was found that the failures that most affect engine efficiency are directly related to the following subsystems: cooling, lubricant, fuel, charge air and exhaust gases. The fault diagnosis method proposed in this work is based on the historical data of the operational variables of the MTU-16V4000-G81 engines in operation. It is important to highlight that in the combustion process the relationships between the variables of boost pressure, fuel temperature, injection quantity, etc. they are non-linear and it is very difficult to determine a model efficiently that seeks to normalize the SFC.

An important contribution to this difficulty is the proposed detection of the incipient deviation of the main parameters that alter the consumption index. A fuzzy method is offered that suggests an operating procedure that meets the objective of a simple and easy to implement solution useful to suggest actions that allow to normalize the specific fuel consumption immediately.

From the study, it was found that the symptoms that most affect the deterioration of the consumption index are the following: cylinder inlet charge air pressure (V1), turbo inlet vacuum (V2), charge air temperature (V3), injection percent (V4), air mass (V5), gas temperature after turbo (V6), consumption (V7) and pressure in the high pressure rail (V8). Its limits are represented in Table 1 for working powers at 75% and 100%, which are the most used values in the database of the SCADA EROS installed in the power plant.

For the location of the main interruptions during the study, it was chosen to identify the faults F1, F2, F3, F4 and F5, so it was decided to add the following input variables: fuel pressure at the engine inlet (V9) and the fuel temperature in the high-pressure rail (V10). These last input variables are the ones that showed the greatest influence on the

Table 1. Limit thresholds of the MTU-16V4000-G81 combustion engine diagnostic variables

V1 (bar)	V2 (mbar)	V3 (°C)	V4 (%)	V5 (mg)	V6 (°C)	V7 (l/min)	V8 (bar)
>2.5	≥30	>35	≤70	≥11500	-	<5.7	≥1200
≥3.2	>45	≥60	≤95	≥12000	≤420	<5.8	≥1300

previous failures, having the limits in V9 (4–7 bar) and V10 (40 °C – 55 °C) at 75% and 100% respectively.

Based on the diagrams designed by the authors in [21, 22], Fig. 2 shows the proposed fuzzy logic based fault diagnosis structure for MTU-16V4000-G81 engines.

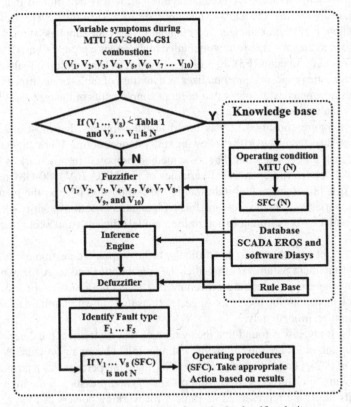

Fig. 2. The flow chart of the fuzzy logic classifier design

The fuzzification process in the input variables was carried out through the construction of triangular membership functions. The fuzzy sets were defined depending on the behavior of the thresholds obtained from the limits described in Table 1. Then, with a rule base, the relationship between the symptoms that are manifested in the measured variables and the occurrence of the failures.

In [23] the authors presented a multiple failure detection scheme in which they cross-validated different sets of membership functions for the same rule base. For the study, real failure cases were used that were compared with different fuzzy membership functions. From the analysis of the diagnostic results, it was confirmed that the trapezoidal function obtained 87.7% accuracy, whereas the triangular, Gaussian and bell functions obtained 85.9%, 81.2% and 83% accuracy, respectively.

Based on the above, the fuzzification process in the symptoms variables of the proposed system is carried out through the construction of trapezoidal membership functions. The fuzzy sets were defined depending on the behavior of the thresholds obtained from the boundary limits of the fault zones that are described in Table 1.

Then, with a rule base, the relationship between the symptoms manifested in the variables measured and the occurrence of failures. They are of the Mamdani type because the outputs are not going to be functions that depend on the inputs, but rather they are going to be fuzzy sets.

If V1 is A_1^1 and V2 is A_2^2 and ... and Vn is A_n^j Then Fault Fs.
Where:

n: is the number of input variables. In our case n = 10 (V1, V2, V3, V4 V5, V6, V7, V8, V9 and V10).
j: is the number of fuzzy sets defined for each symptom variable. In our case, j = 5. Very low (Mf1), low (Mf2), normal (Mf3), high (Mf4) and very high (Mf5) as shown in the example of Fig. 3(a).
s: is the number of SFC conditions analyzed. In our case s = 4 (C1, C2, C3 and C4).

For the particular case of the output variables, look for the identification of the faults, s = 5, is the number of faults analyzed. In our case (F1, F2, F3, F4 and F5).

All the input variables of the FDIp are represented by membership functions that are defined through the fuzzy sets (Mf1, Mf2, Mf3, Mf4 and Mf5) as shown in the example of Fig. 3(a) for the case cylinder inlet charge air pressure. Figure 3(b) shows the fuzzification of the SFC condition. Four types of conditions are considered in this output variable: Satisfactory or normal (C1), above normal (C2), high consumption (C3) and very high consumption (C4). The four fuzzy sets at the output are in the range 0 to 8 as shown in Fig. 3(b).

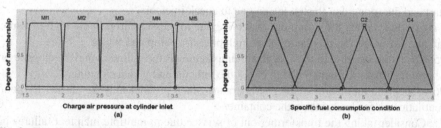

Fig. 3. Fuzzification process of the variables of the proposed method. (a) Fuzzification of the cylinder input charge air pressure input variable; (b) Fuzzification of combustion engine failures.

All the rules used in this investigation were given the same order of operation. They are of the Mamdani type and their design is such that when a data point is in the identification zones: F1, F2, F3 or F4, a single fault is diagnosed. In case the data point belongs within F5, then Fm are diagnosed.

The proposal, based on fuzzy rules, determines the condition of specific fuel consumption in an incipient way. It allows suggesting maintenance actions by monitoring the limits of all input variables. Figure 4(a) shows the fuzzification for the fault output case. In this output variable, five types of conditions are considered in the single fault category F1, F2, F3 and F4 and one fault in the multiple fault category (F5).

The latter represents the mixture of two more simultaneous simple failures or a simple overall failure with the incipient deviation of the consumption index. The five fuzzy sets that represent the output of the proposed method are located in the range from 0 to 10. Figure 2(b) shows the fuzzification of all the actions to be suggested located in the range from 0 to 14.

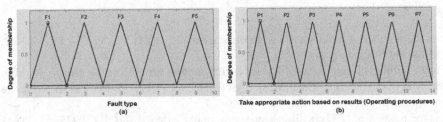

Fig. 4. Fuzzification process of the fault output variables and actions to normalize the SFC. (a) Fuzzification of the types of failure; (b) Fuzzification of operating procedures.

Each of the actions represents the output variables that are described in the following six operating procedures:

P1: Normal operation.

P2: Act with caution, analyze the increase in charge air pressure individually and check the turbo to clean it.

P3: Act with caution, analyze all the parameters that have an impact on the fuel injection system, say: low pressure in the high pressure rail, requested amount of fuel and injection start and duration, plan to stop the engine to check injectors.

P4: Consider taking the group out of service due to pressure drop in the high-pressure rail and check the rail regulator valve, high pressure pump and filters

P5: Check the increase in the charge air temperature as the radiators may be clogged or deteriorated. It is recommended to check the radiator and plan a cleaning.

P6: Check the ambient/container temperature since product may be caused by poor ventilation or gas leaks inside the container.

P7: Consider taking the transformer out of service due to multiple incipient failures in different subsystems and deterioration of the SFC.

With this method, depending on the condition of the transformer, corrective actions are recommended to improve preventive maintenance management and normalize specific fuel consumption.

3 Results and Discussion

To validate the design method, MATLAB® software R2018a was used through simulink. For this, a total of 143 fault data samples were used, distributed as follows: 13 (F1), 53 (F2), 27 (F3), 18 (F4) and 32 (F5). All the cases analyzed come from measurements during the operation of the EG at 75% of its power supply capacity.

Although good fault classification results are obtained, this work recommends including the charge air and exhaust gas cooling subsystems to reduce fault interpretation errors (E) in the proposal. This topic is currently being developed by the authors of this research. The results that are represented in Table 2 show that the FDIp has a good level of accuracy in the identification of simple faults of small magnitude and a good performance in the detection of multiple incipient faults.

Table 2. Accuracy in identifying the failures of the diagnostic proposal

Fault	Description of the fault	Total cases	Proposed method	
			E	Accuracy (%)
F1	High pressure pump malfunction	13	2	84.6
F2	Coolant leak	53	3	94.3
F3	Incorrect spraying of injectors	27	2	92.6
F4	Fuel filter failure	18	5	72.2
F5	Simultaneous occurrence of simple faults	32	1	96.9

The proposed method was able to identify failures in the high pressure pump in 84.6%, leakage of the coolant in 94.3%, in the injectors in 92.6%, in the fuel filters in 72.2% and 96.9% in the incipient detection of multiple failures.

In Fig. 5 the location of a real fault detected in the MTU-16V4000-G81 group motor on 07/29/2020 can be seen. The analysis was carried out by the specialists in industrial maintenance and diagnosis from GEYSEL corresponding to the Technical Department in one of the power plants. In it, engine parameters were downloaded through the MDEC in the working regimes of 75% and 100% load.

For the simulink analysis, only the 75% parameters were taken into account. Figure 5 demonstrated the feasibility of the diagnostic proposal since it allowed the identification of high fuel consumption and consequently an incipient deterioration of the consumption rate during combustion and a high percentage of fuel injection. Given this difficulty, the proposed method suggested stopping the engine to check the injectors. In this way, the diagnostic proposal complies with the solution of a simple method that allows suggesting actions to normalize the specific fuel consumption.

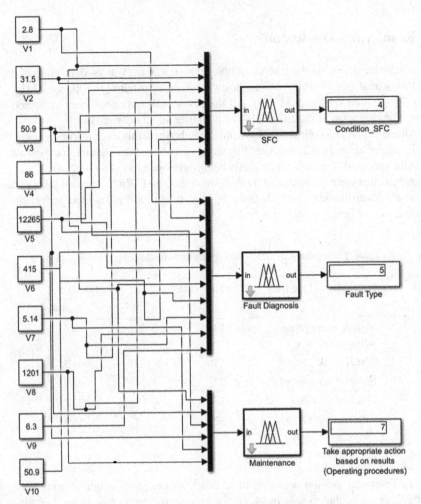

Fig. 5. Simulink model for the fuzzy proposed approach

The results of the proposed method constitute a starting point for further studies in the diagnosis of failures in combustion engines that are present in the MTU-16V4000-G81 generating sets based on fuzzy logic. Also, it is simple and practical, not as complicated as SVM, ANN, and other smart algorithms described in [5–8] and in [9, 10]. The generalization of this method is the object of study in the rest of the MTU type engines that have supercharging and with few adjustments it can be adapted to engines that do not have this system.

Aspects such as robustness is a topic of great importance for the development of current diagnostic methods and constitutes an insufficiency in this research. Although the fuzzy logic proposal showed high sensitivity, being able to quickly detect incipient faults in the studied combustion engine. However, depending on the type of application in industrial processes, this proposal could be affected by the effect of external disturbances or noise; making it difficult to correctly distinguish the faults that have occurred.

In these cases, the techniques used must be robust in these situations without implying losing precision in the identification of failures. The development of future research by the authors is aimed at improving the robustness of the diagnostic tool by incorporating a method as a pre-processing stage to isolate the noise that may be present in the measurements.

4   Conclusions

In this work, a method for fault diagnosis was designed and tested using fuzzy logic in MTU-16V4000-G81 combustion engines. This technique has been found to be very useful in improving the accuracy of failure analysis and enhancing the ability to detect multiple incipient failures.

The proposed failure diagnosis method, based on historical data, achieved the detection of multiple failures in 96.9% and a total accuracy rate of 88.1%, demonstrating its feasibility.

The proposal offers a method to determine the incipient deviation of the main parameters that alter the consumption index. It offered a fuzzy method that suggests an operating procedure based on a set of actions to normalize the specific fuel consumption.

Its validation results showed that there is a simple, low-complexity and easy-to-implement solution for the analysis of incipient failures in combustion engines.

Acknowledgements. The authors appreciate the collaboration of the members of the Research Project: Advanced Automation for the Elaboration and Refinement of Steels (AA-ELACERO) - Code: P211LH021-023 financed by the Stainless Steel Company, ACINOX, Las Tunas in Cuba. We thank the specialists of the Electric and Automatic Group at ACINOX. We are very grateful to the Department of Operations (GEYSEL), for guaranteeing the necessary resources to carry out this research.

References

1. Singh, A.K., Saxena, A., Roy, N., Choudhury, U.: Inter-turn fault stability enrichment and diagnostic analysis of power system network using wavelet transformation-based sample data control and fuzzy logic controller. Trans. Inst. Meas. Control (2021). https://doi.org/10.1177/01423312211007006
2. Kang, J., Lu, Y., Luo, H., Li, J., Hou, Y., Zhang, Y.: Wear assessment model for cylinder liner of internal combustion engine under fuzzy uncertainty. Mech. Ind. **22**, 29 (2021). https://doi.org/10.1051/meca/2021028
3. Hadroug, N., Hafaifa, A., Alili, B., Iratni, A., Chen, X.: Fuzzy diagnostic strategy implementation for gas turbine vibrations faults detection: towards a characterization of symptom–fault correlations. J. Vibr. Eng. Technol. 1–27 (2021). https://doi.org/10.1007/s42417-021-00373-z

4. Yazdani, S., Montazeri-Gh, M.: A novel gas turbine fault detection and identification strategy based on hybrid dimensionality reduction and uncertain rule-based fuzzy logic. Comput. Ind. **115**, 103131 (2021). https://doi.org/10.1016/j.compind.2019.103131

5. Shahbaz, M.H., Amin, A.A.: Design of active fault tolerant control system for air fuel ratio control of internal combustion engines using artificial neural networks. IEEE Access **9**, 46022–46032 (2021). https://doi.org/10.1109/ACCESS.2021.3068164

6. Bhatt, A.N., Shrivastava, N.: Application of artificial neural network for internal combustion engines: a state of the art review. Arch. Comput. Methods Eng. 1–23 (2021). https://doi.org/10.1007/s11831-021-09596-5

7. Khazaee, M., Banakar, A., Ghobadian, B., Mirsalim, M.A., Minaei, S.: Remaining useful life (RUL) prediction of internal combustion engine timing belt based on vibration signals and artificial neural network. Neural Comput. Appl. **33**(13), 7785–7801 (2020). https://doi.org/10.1007/s00521-020-05520-3

8. da Silva Junior, E.M., de Sousa, D.R., Marinho, L.C.R.P., Formiga, C.R.B., Matamoros, E.P.: Fault diagnosis in combustion engines using artificial neural networks. SAE Technical Paper 2020-36-0076 (2021). https://doi.org/10.4271/2020-36-0076

9. Zhang, M., Zi, Y., Niu, L., Xi, S., Li, Y.: Intelligent diagnosis of V-type marine diesel engines based on multifeatures extracted from instantaneous crankshaft speed. IEEE Trans. Instrum. Meas. **68**(3), 722–740 (2018). https://doi.org/10.1109/TIM.2018.2857018

10. Jafarian, K., Mobin, M., Jafari-Marandi, R., Rabiei, E.: Misfire and valve clearance faults detection in the combustion engines based on a multi-sensor vibration signal monitoring. Measurement **128**, 527–536 (2018). https://doi.org/10.1016/j.measurement.2018.04.062

11. Abdelrahim, E.M.: Hierarchical adaptive genetic algorithm based T–S fuzzy controller for non-linear automotive applications. Int. J. Fuzzy Syst. 1–15 (2021). https://doi.org/10.1007/s40815-021-01153-3

12. Cai, B., et al.: Fault detection and diagnostic method of diesel engine by combining rule-based algorithm and BNs/BPNNs. J. Manuf. Syst. **57**, 148–157 (2020). https://doi.org/10.1016/j.jmsy.2020.09.001

13. Gai, J., Hu, Y.: Research on fault diagnosis based on singular value decomposition and fuzzy neural network. Shock Vibr. (2018). https://doi.org/10.1155/2018/8218657

14. Babichev, S., Strielkovskaya, L., Zaitsev, O., Khamula, O.: Development of a fuzzy inference model for the management of a marine engine. In: Babichev, S., Lytvynenko, V., Wójcik, W., Vyshemyrskaya, S. (eds.) ISDMCI 2020. AISC, vol. 1246, pp. 331–340. Springer, Cham (2021). https://doi.org/10.1007/978-3-030-54215-3_21

15. Looney, B.: Statistical Review of World Energy, 69th edn. BP, London, UK (2020)

16. Dean Labrada, A., Ponce Iglesias, R., Torres Breffe, O.E., Espinosa Domínguez, J., Caballero Mena, Á.J.: Modificaciones al Relé NSR 376 SA para Grupos Electrógenos de la Tecnología MTU. Ingeniería Energética **42**(2), 81–89 (2021)

17. Karatuğ, Ç., Arslanoğlu, Y.: Importance of early fault diagnosis for marine diesel engines: a case study on efficiency management and environment. Ships Offshore Struct. 1–9 (2020). https://doi.org/10.1080/17445302.2020.1835077

18. Corrales Barrios, L., Ramírez Vázquez, A.: Clasificación de fallas con redes neuronales para grupos electrógenos. Ingeniería Energética **34**(2), 137–150 (2013)

19. Song, E., Ke, Y., Yao, C., Dong, Q., Yang, L.: Fault diagnosis method for high-pressure common rail injector based on IFOA-VMD and hierarchical dispersion entropy. Entropy **21**(10), 923 (2019). https://doi.org/10.3390/e21100923

20. Álvarez Kile, P., Díaz Concepción, A., Rodríguez Piñeiro, A.J., Guillén García, J., Guillén García, J.G., Alfonso Álvarez, A.: Causas de la desviación del índice de consumo de combustible en los generadores eléctricos Hyundai. Ingeniería Energética **41**(2) (2020)

21. Fernández, J.C., Corrales, L.B., Hernández, F.H., Benítez, I.F., Núñez, J.R.: A fuzzy logic proposal for diagnosis multiple incipient faults in a power transformer. In: Hernández Heredia, Y., Milián Núñez, V., Ruiz Shulcloper, J. (eds.) IWAIPR 2021. LNCS, vol. 13055, pp. 187–198. Springer, Cham (2021). https://doi.org/10.1007/978-3-030-89691-1_19

22. Fernández Blanco, J.C., Hernández González, F.H., Corrales Barrios, L.B.: Método de lógica difusa para el diagnóstico de fallos incipientes en un transformador de 40MVA. Ingeniería Electrónica, Automática y Comunicaciones **42**(2), 76–88 (2021)

23. Wani, S.A., Gupta, D., Farooque, M.U., Khan, S.A.: Multiple incipient fault classification approach for enhancing the accuracy of dissolved gas analysis (DGA). IET Sci. Meas. Technol. **13**(7), 959–967 (2019). https://doi.org/10.1049/iet-smt.2018.5135

DDoS Attack Preventing and Detection with the Artificial Intelligence Approach

Tariqul Islam$^{(\boxtimes)}$, Md. Ismail Jabiullah$^{(\boxtimes)}$, and Dm. Mehedi Hasan Abid$^{(\boxtimes)}$

Daffodil International University, Dhaka, Bangladesh
{tariqul15-2250,drismail.cse,mehedi15-226}@diu.edu.bd

Abstract. DDoS attacks are a major Internet security concern with this large number of customers. Each attack sends a service request to a certain server, which limits the server's capacity to provide normal services. Since the attackers use legitimate packages and alter their package information, traditional methods are not very effective. The assault on DDoS is one of the most potent Internet hacking techniques. The hacker's basic weapon to take down and crash websites during these sorts of assaults is network trafficking. There are different sub-categories, each category explains how a hacker attempts to enter the network. In this paper, we define the DDoS attacks detection method based on artificial intelligence and explored with more than 96-percent accuracy a technique to detect a DDoS attacks assault danger using artificial intelligence (A.I). In addition to a secure or healthy network, authors have identified 7 separate sub-categories of DDoS attacks.

Keywords: DDoS · Cyber security · Artificial intelligence · Neural networks · Data visualization · Data analytics

1 Introduction

The DDoS attack uses many distributed resource contra targets which will deprive authorized clients of service [1, 2]. DDoS attacks generate large volumes of traffic in a small time [3]. DDoS attacks can have a big impact on victims. Two types of DDoS attacks are IP spoofing, other is Flooding attacks. IP spoofing and Flooding attack differences are respectively impersonating a trusted source, sending exceeding packets to disrupt the services [4]. Also, DDoS attacks have three kinds of different flooding attacks [5, 6]. It is possible to use ML classification methods to differentiate between good and bad packages. Bayes classifiers are used in ML classification methods based upon the application of the Bayes theorem [7]. ANN can communicate with neurons and solve problems like the brain that is used in security fields [8]. Attack aims to jam the excessive traffic on the network or server. It is successful by the use, as a source of the attack, of several hacked systems. "SYN Flood, UDP Flood, MSSQL, LDAP, Portmap, NetBIOS" are among the sub-categories we identified via our study. Machine learning is one of the most frequent backbones of AI day. We utilize address issues with precise human performance in different fields. We have evaluated the A.I. boundaries once again to discover the dangers in the field of cyber safety. In this study, the logs that were created

© Springer Nature Switzerland AG 2022
C. Brito-Loeza et al. (Eds.): ISICS 2022, CCIS 1569, pp. 30–43, 2022.
https://doi.org/10.1007/978-3-030-98457-1_3

during a DDoS assault were thoroughly analyzed using supervised and non-controlled threat detection approaches. Finally, we utilized deep learning to achieve more accuracy than 96-percent for classification and safe connection for distinct types of DDoS threats.

2 Related Work

In this paper, Zhang et al. [9] describe that in last year's many DDoS attacks launched at a minimum cost. The cause says that DDoS attacks traffic is the same as normal traffic. Some ML algorithms are able to classify and detect traffic of DDoS attacks. They survey new papers on DDoS attack detection progress. Here [3] proposes NN (Neural network) based DDoS attacks detection that has five phases. They store traffic data in Hadoop distributed systems to detect DDoS attacks. The paper [4] proposes a mitigation model by ML algorithm for DDoS attacks detection. OMS for composing the model and monitoring DDoS attacks impact measurements. This model performance is increased than other ML algorithms. Authors [10] develop NN based DDoS attacks detection systems. Here [5] authors design an ANN-based model for detection of DDoS DNS amplification attacks. Ndibwile et al. [11] propose a network architecture for servers to distinguish DDoS attack traffic. Supervised learning machine-learning algorithm for customizing the ISP network gateway and decision tree used for malicious traffic, the random tree algorithm also used for avoiding false-positive traffic. Fouladi et al. [12] propose a frequency analysis method for detection, DWT gives the best accuracy but some features extracted from DWT and DFT then increase the accuracy of detection. Ramadan et al. [6] design an AIS system for flood attacks detection. There are four different phases of DCA (Dendritic cell algorithm). Peraković et al. [13] develop an ANN-based detection system, In ANN (Artificial Neural Network) model, traffics are classified into 4 types. The classification accuracy of UDP DDoS attacks is slightly lower than that of normal traffic. Kushnir et al. [14] propose an approach to enable completely automated. The solution is applicable with minimal configuration effort to a wide range of web applications without requiring access to the source code and without requiring the availability of a formal access control model. Our evaluation demonstrates that the solution can indeed be applied to various types of web applications. There are some limitations such as Focus on getting Requests and Evaluation scope is limited with four simple websites. Man et al. [15] Proposed a detecting method like distributed vulnerability, which method to improve the system performance and efficiency for large Java Web programs. Some limitations are that the model only exploits vulnerabilities that are supported by American Fuzzy lop (such as Code Execution, Denial-of-service, etc.)". Model elements are targeted when the program decomposes, worker nodes perform guided fuzzing, and master nodes perform symbolic execution, creating constraint condition input for the test program. The result parameters are the efficiency of fuzzing and program coverage. Anagandula et al. [15] review the performance of 4 black box web- application scanners for store SQL, XSS vulnerability at the well-known testbed (i.e. Wackopicko, Scan it) by three renowned scanners i.e. Wireshark, Burp Suite, and Nessus. Al Jumuah et al. [16] they developed a six-stage algorithm and used chaos theory to efficiently detect DDoS attacks. A mirror image of an actual network environment is used to initiate the learning process. The authors launched various DDoS attacks while legitimate traffic flows across the network. They distinguished DDoS attacks from real traffic using supervised and unsupervised ANN methods. They used up-to-date datasets and formed artificial neural networks into two learning methods and achieved over 95% accuracy in detecting DDoS attacks. In this paper [17], the authors propose hybrid ML model. They show results the hybrid ML model gives us good accuracy with detection rate compared to other normal ML models. Alzahrani et al. [18] propose detecting known and unknown DDoS Attacks systems, apply different IDS approaches, anomaly-based distributed ANN and signature-based approaches. This research paper [19] reviews the DDoS attacks survey to prevent recognition by data mining and use it to identify DDOS attack patterns and analyze patterns with ML algorithms. The result give the best accuracy by data mining algorithms for preventing DDoS attacks. Ghafarian et al. [20] present a platform-independent hybrid method without including further defensive code in the application. Mohammadi et al. [21] present a method for detecting vulnerabilities considerably earlier in the development cycle, as well as providing detailed feedback to developers on how to repair the flaw. The test evaluation is based on execution behavior, which can detect subtle vulnerabilities originating from internal browser decoding functions, and this method works with all currently available web languages. Ibarra-flallos et al. [22] design a durable, reliable, and effective protection filter for reducing common web injection attacks. The author proposes a regular expressions-based input field validation filter and a sanitization method. Figueiredo et al. [23] developed a learning-based tool that is able to detect input validation vulnerability from the source code of a web application using static data flow analysis. This paper limitation is research focused on the PHP and Java Source Code, the study did not compare their outcome with other dictation tools, and MERLIN only considered the input validation vulnerability attack. Kao et al. [24] The paper provides an in-depth examination of the many types of SQLi assaults, their descriptions, and possible investigation strategies. However, there are significant limitations, such as the possible impact on SQL injection investigations and the examination of practical uses of the SIA framework in legal procedures, and the framework's accuracy is not thoroughly evaluated. Mokbal et al. [25] present large real-world data made up of 138,569 unique records for detecting XSS threats that has been built fully and distinctively. To offer training and testing datasets, a dynamic features extraction method is presented to extract data from a neural network model. When employed against XSS assaults, this approach is more resilient and platform-independent. The authors [26] during the session hijacking attack in VANETs, the main focus is on recognizing the malicious node that poses as a valid vehicle. The main focus of this research is on preventative approaches for deliberately hidden nodes. It does not, however, address security concerns such as message confidentiality and privacy. In this paper [27] the implications of SATs' actions while analyzing applications written in various coding styles and programming methods, as well as a discussion of the exploitability of SQLi vulnerabilities reported by SATs as true positives. Some result parameters are "TP, FP, FN, FFP (False False Positive)". Here [28] authors propose an LVQ neural network for host anomaly detection that uses the DDoS attacks detection method. That can improve the recognition rate of the detection system. Yuan et al. [29] investigate vulnerabilities analyze common web application vulnerabilities, research the basic characteristics of these vulnerabilities in depth, and comprehend the principles and remedies to these weaknesses. Moustafa et al. [30] suggest a method to automatically extract relevant features from web data and network traffic data to improve the effectiveness of threat detection techniques.

3 Research Methodology

3.1 Preprocessing Data

One of our initial problems has been the processing of data cause it [31] contained 88 characteristics. It was a really difficult challenge for us to process this enormous data inside a restricted RAM capacity. So, we lowered the attribute data type, hence reducing the data framework's memory use. Float64 data types have been reduced to "float32, int64 to int32, int32 to uint32" etc. Nearly 42% of the initial size has been decreased. The qualities or characteristics of our database were still almost unlimited, therefore, we also processed these data at the preprocessing stage. For instruments used throughout this research TensorFlow, Scikit Learn, Matplotlib, Seaborn.

3.2 The Distribution of Target Features

It can be observed that we have attempted to keep the goal feature evenly distributed together with the data set. While UDPLag is rather unequal in distribution to others, this situation has nevertheless been dealt with later on in this study (Fig. 1).

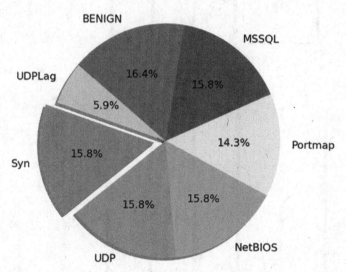

Fig. 1. Target features

3.3 Data Analysis

Data analysis is the process of examining and describing a huge number of data points with care. This element of the research process is usually completed in stages [32]. Typically, researchers collect data during the whole data collection procedure. The purpose of this step is to identify the patterns and procedures that will allow them to examine the data. To preserve the integrity of the data, it is critical to strictly follow the norms and procedures for statistical analysis (Fig. 2).

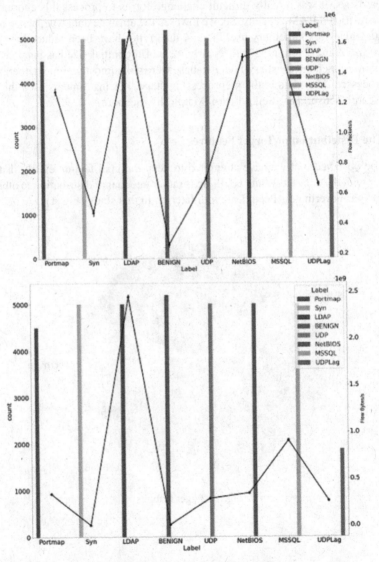

Fig. 2. The bit and packet flow drift

In the two above assessments, bit and packet flow drift in a DDoS assault in comparison with a Benign or a Security connection may be observed (Fig. 3).

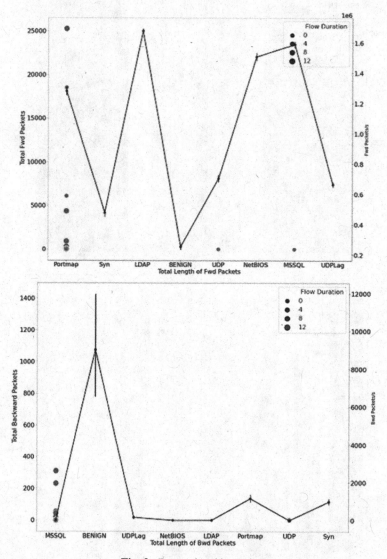

Fig. 3. Protocol and incoming

In each kind of protocol and incoming, we have also studied the distribution of each threat category. The diagrams showing the analysis are shown below (Fig. 4).

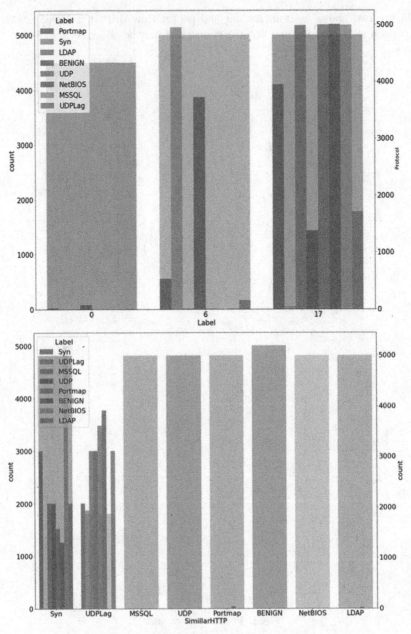

Fig. 4. Threat analysis

4 The Approach for Detection of the Threat in Unsupervised Method

In our unsupervised method, we don't allow our model to learn from the target variables, but instead force our algorithms to know from the input data. Before training, pre-processing. Some of the functions of our data have been deleted. "Flow Packets" and "Flow Bytes/s" have been deleted as they have been converted to excessively big values for float64 and NaN after normal scaling. By conventional scaling and normalization, we have scaled our data. Use the main dimension, reduction-component analysis, and decrease the size to two-dimensional data (Fig. 5).

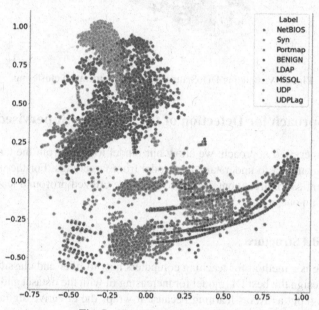

Fig. 5. Visualizing DDoS attacks

Thus, it can be readily noticed from the above two visualizations that the distinct threats may be clustered in some way by our method. See how the produced clusters might be identified with our unattended model (Fig. 6).

It seems that our uncontrolled model has successfully identified a trend in the data and could to some extent segment our target variable. Non-controlled learning provides a detailed perspective of the data's shape and structure, as well as analysis. If the form and structure of the data change as they are not informed of the target information, the prediction of the grouping and the label of the target will vary. No way controlled machine learning is better adapted to real-life situations and It's not accurate. It is also one of the reasons that uncontrolled formed models are not adapted to production deployments.

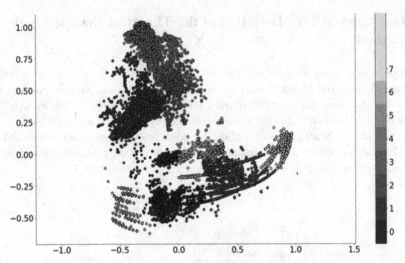

Fig. 6. Visualizing DDoS attacks after agglomerative clustering

5   The Approach for Detection of the Threat in Supervised Method

Unlike the supervised approach, we allow our model to learn from the target variable that allows our model to understand the model from target tags. For the unsupervised approach, identical pretreatment data were used. We utilized profound learning in this example to train our model.

5.1   DL Model Structure

Deep learning is a method for teaching computers how to filter and classify data. Here our authors design the best DL model for increasing fit with the dataset and input given. Authors give input as Keras learning because it wraps the effective digital computing libraries TensorFlow and allows you to define and form neural network models (Fig. 7).

As our objective variable was unbalanced, a stratified K-fold was used to form and assess our data on each fold. The distribution of training and the validation of an unbalanced feature is balanced. To evaluate the model's performance, we used Adam as the base optimizer and ROC AUC. An area where the ROC AUC score is calculated from the prediction scores below the characteristic curve of the recipient. We developed and validated our 10-step model and achieved ROC Auc scores of 96% or more on an average of 97% or more for threat detection (Fig. 8).

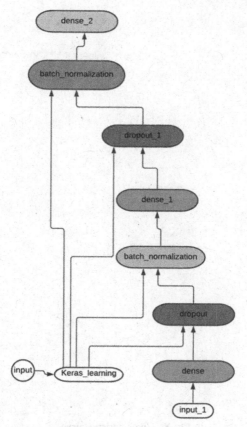

Fig. 7. The DL model

6 Result

The evaluation procedure' results were achieved using 10-fold cross-validation. This technique ensures that the data is never from the same person. A different split of the original sample is used each time the test and training data are used.

In Table 1, Syn was detected with greatest precision, recall, and f1-score of 99 percent false positives per volume in Table 1, resulting in a positive prediction. On a 2.2 GHz dual-core laptop computer, the whole processing time was between 9.9 and 13.0 s on average, with the majority of the time spent on disk candidate discovery.

Precision refers to everything that is relevant, whereas recall refers to everything that is genuinely relevant. The recall of your model is also known as its sensitivity, whereas precision is known as Positive Predicted Value. The precision of the Table 2 discovered folds classification has been justified.

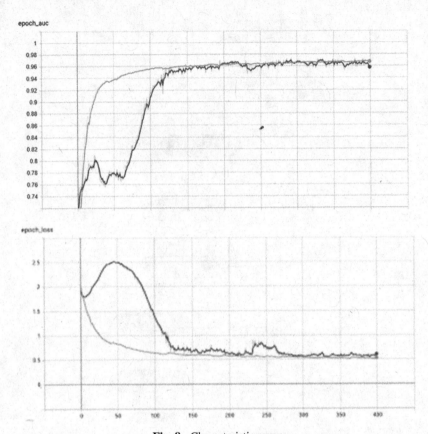

Fig. 8. Characteristic curve

Table 1. Ten folds classifications report

	Precision	Recall	f1-score	Support
BENIGN	0.98	0.99	0.98	519
Portmap	0.94	0.97	0.96	500
NetBIOS	0.86	0.85	0.86	500
LDAP	0.60	0.90	0.72	500
UDP	0.91	0.10	0.18	500
Syn	0.99	0.99	0.99	500
MSSQL	0.66	0.75	0.70	500
UDPLag	0.55	0.88	0.67	188
Accuracy			0.80	3707
Macro avg	0.81	0.80	0.76	3707
Weighted avg	0.83	0.80	0.77	3707

Table 2. Ten folds classifications report

	Accuracy
BENIGN	0.97687861
Portmap	0.206
NetBIOS	0.96
LDAP	0.862
UDP	0.138
Syn	0.982
MSSQL	0.498
UDPLag	0.91489362

7 Conclusion

In this paper authors have relatively little labeled data in the real situation compared to unlabeled data, there are ways to achieve amazing performance, such as semi-monitored learning and self-management. The Model Fairness Indicator may also be used as one of the TensorFlow tools to improve model assessment and performance scaling. The authors have identified 7 separate sub-categories of DDoS attacks threats. And we get 96-percent accuracy to detect DDoS attacks and assault danger using artificial intelligence.

References

1. Yuan, X., Li, C., Li, X.: DeepDefense: identifying DDoS attack via deep learning. In: 2017 IEEE International Conference on Smart Computing (SMARTCOMP), Hong Kong, 2017, pp. 1–8 (2017). https://doi.org/10.1109/SMARTCOMP.2017.7946998
2. Guri, M., Mirsky, Y., Elovici, Y.: 9-1-1 DDoS: attacks, analysis and mitigation. In: 2017 IEEE European Symposium on Security and Privacy (EuroS&P), Paris, France, 2017, pp. 218–232 (2017). https://doi.org/10.1109/EuroSP.2017.23
3. Hsieh, C.J., Chan, T.Y.: Detection DDoS attacks based on neural-network using Apache Spark. In: 2016 International Conference on Applied System Innovation (ICASI), Okinawa, 2016, pp. 1–4 (2016). https://doi.org/10.1109/ICASI.2016.7539833
4. Kiruthika Devi, B.S., Preetha, G., Selvaram, G., Mercy Shalinie, S.: An impact analysis: real time DDoS attack detection and mitigation using machine learning. In: 2014 International Conference on Recent Trends in Information Technology, Chennai, 2014, pp. 1–7 (2014). https://doi.org/10.1109/ICRTIT.2014.6996133
5. Meitei, I.L., Singh, K.J., De, T.: Detection of DDoS DNS amplification attack using classification algorithm. In: Proceedings of the International Conference on Informatics and Analytics (ICIA-16), Article 81, p. 6. ACM, New York, NY, The USA (2016). https://doi.org/10.1145/2980258.2980431
6. Ramadhan, G., Kurniawan, Y., Kim, C.-S.: Design of TCP SYN flood DDoS attack detection using artificial immune systems. In: 2016 6th International Conference on System Engineering and Technology (ICSET), Bandung, 2016, pp. 72–76 (2016). https://doi.org/10.1109/ICSEngT.2016.7849626

7. Rish, I.: An empirical study of the naive Bayes classifier. J. Univ. Comput. Sci. **1**(2), 127 (2001)
8. Ahmad, I., Abdullah, A.B., Alghamdi, A.S.: Artificial neural network approaches to intrusion detection: a review. In: WSEAS International Conference on Telecommunications and Informatics World Scientific and Engineering Academy and Society (WSEAS), pp. 200–205 (2009)
9. Zhang, B., Tao, Z., Yu, Z.: DDoS detection and prevention based on artificial intelligence techniques. In: 2017 3rd IEEE International Conference on Computer and Communications (ICCC). IEEE (2017)
10. Zhao, T., Lo, D.C.T., Qian, K.: A neural-network based DDoS detection system using hadoop and HBase. In: 2015 IEEE 17th International Conference on High Performance Computing and Communications, 2015 IEEE 7th International Symposium on Cyberspace Safety and Security, and 2015 IEEE 12th International Conference on Embedded Software and Systems, New York, NY, 2015, pp. 1326–1331 (2015). https://doi.org/10.1109/HPCC-CSS-ICESS.201 5.38
11. Ndibwile, J.D., Govardhan, A., Okada, K., Kadobayashi,Y.: Web server protection against application layer DDoS attacks using machine learning and traffic authentication. In: 2015 IEEE 39th Annual Computer Software and Applications Conference, Taichung, 2015, pp. 261–267 (2015). https://doi.org/10.1109/COMPSAC.2015.240
12. Fouladi, R.F., Kayatas, C.E., Anarim, E.: Frequency based DDoS attack detection approach using naive Bayes classification. In: 2016 39th International Conference on Telecommunications and Signal Processing (TSP), Vienna, 2016, pp. 104–107 (2016). https://doi.org/10.1109/TSP.2016.7760838
13. Peraković, D., Periša, M., Cvitić, I., Husnjak, S.: Artificial neuron network implementation in detection and classification of DDoS traffic. In: 2016 24th Telecommunications Forum (TELFOR), Belgrade, pp. 1–4 (2016). https://doi.org/10.1109/TELFOR.2016.7818791
14. Kushnir, M., et al.: Automated black box detection of HTTP GET request-based access control vulnerabilities in web applications. In: Man, H., et al. (eds.) ICISSP 2021, JSEFuzz: Vulnerability Detection Method for Java Web Application. 2018 3rd International Conference on System Reliability and Safety (ICSRS), Online 11–13 February 2021. SciTePress (2021)
15. Anagandula, K., Zavarsky, P.: An analysis of effectiveness of black-box web application scanners in detection of stored SQL injection and stored XSS vulnerabilities. In: 2020 3rd International Conference on Data Intelligence and Security (ICDIS). IEEE (2020)
16. Aljumah, A., Ahamad, T.: A novel approach for detecting DDoS using artificial neural networks. Int. J. Comput. Sci. Netw. Secur. **16**(12), 132–138 (2016)
17. Deepa, V., Muthamil Sudar, K., Deepalakshmi, P.: Detection of DDoS attack on SDN control plane using hybrid machine learning techniques. In: 2018 International Conference on Smart Systems and Inventive Technology (ICSSIT). IEEE (2018)
18. Alzahrani, S., Hong, L.: Detection of Distributed Denial of Service (DDoS) attacks using artificial intelligence on cloud. In: 2018 IEEE World Congress on Services (SERVICES), pp. 35–36 (2018). https://doi.org/10.1109/SERVICES.2018.00031
19. Bandara, K.R.W.V., et al.: Preventing DDOS attack using data mining algorithms. Int. J. Sci. Res. Publ. **6**(10), 390 (2016)
20. Ghafarian, A.: A hybrid method for detection and prevention of SQL injection attacks. In: 2017 Computing Conference. IEEE (2017)
21. Mohammadi, M., et al.: Automatic web security unit testing: XSS vulnerability detection. In: 2016 IEEE/ACM 11th International Workshop in Automation of Software Test (AST). IEEE (2016)
22. Ibarra-Fiallos, S., et al.: Effective filter for common injection attacks in online web applications. IEEE Access **9**, 10378–10391 (2021)

23. Figueiredo, A., Lide, T., Correia, M.: Multi-language web vulnerability detection. In: 2020 IEEE International Symposium on Software Reliability Engineering Workshops (ISSREW). IEEE (2020)

24. Kao, D.-Y., Lai, C.-J., Su, C.-W.: A framework for SQL injection investigations: detection, investigation, and forensics. In: 2018 IEEE International Conference on Systems, Man, and Cybernetics (SMC). IEEE (2018)

25. Mokbal, F.M.M., et al.: MLPXSS: an integrated XSS-based attack detection scheme in web applications using multilayer perceptron technique. IEEE Access **7**, 100567–100580 (2019)

26. Jeevitha, R., Sudha Bhuvaneswari, N.: Malicious node detection in VANET session hijacking attack. In: 2019 IEEE International Conference on Electrical, Computer and Communication Technologies (ICECCT). IEEE (2019)

27. Medeiros, I., Neves, N.: Effect of coding styles in detection of web application vulnerabilities. In: 2020 16th European Dependable Computing Conference (EDCC). IEEE (2020)

28. Li, J., Liu, Y., Lin, G.: DDoS attack detection based on a neural network. In: 2010 2nd International Symposium on Aware Computing. IEEE (2010)

29. Yuan, H., et al.: Research and implementation of security vulnerability detection in application system of WEB static source code analysis based on JAVA. In: Xu, Z., Choo, K.K., Dehghantanha, A., Parizi, R., Hammoudeh, M. (eds.) The International Conference on Cyber Security Intelligence and Analytics, pp. 444–452. Springer, Cham (2019). https://doi.org/10.1007/978-3-030-15235-2_66

30. Moustafa, N., Misra, G., Slay, J.: Generalized outlier Gaussian mixture technique based on automated association features for simulating and detecting web application attacks. IEEE Trans. Sustain. Comput. (2018)

31. The UNIVERSITY OF New BRUNSWICK DDoS evaluation dataset (CIC-DDoS2019). https://www.unb.ca/cic/datasets/ddos-2019.html

32. Shamoo, A.E., Resnik, D.B.: Responsible Conduct of Research. Oxford University Press, Oxford (2009)

Iris Recognition Using Supervised Learning Based on Matching Features

Edgar Hernandez-Garcia, Anabel Martin-Gonzalez$^{(\boxtimes)}$ ⓘ,
and Ricardo Legarda-Saenz ⓘ

Computational Learning and Imaging Research, Facultad de Matemáticas,
Universidad Autónoma de Yucatán, 97205 Merida, Mexico
{amarting,rlegarda}@correo.uady.mx

Abstract. Biometrics is a discipline that studies methods for verification and identification of individuals based on physical or behavioral characteristics of a person. In this paper, an iris recognition system is proposed using supervised learning based on statistical features of matching points obtained from speeded up robust features, which are invariant to transformations. Our system extracts statistics from correspondence patterns between the pair of iris images to be compared to generate an efficient feature vector. A set of these feature vectors, obtained from several iris samples, feeds a learning algorithm to automatically classify whether the pair of images corresponds to the same iris. To evaluate the recognition rate of our system, we performed experiments on the CASIA iris image database, obtaining a recognition rate of 99.94%, with a False Acceptance Rate (FAR) of 0.00%, and a False Rejection Rate (FRR) of 0.12%, which shows efficient classification rates; moreover, this model achieves the fastest computational (1.18 s) time compared to other iris recognition methods.

Keywords: Iris recognition · Supervised learning · Matching-based features · Speeded up robust features · Pattern recognition

1 Introduction

Identity verification and identification is a common practice nowadays to enhance security and to maintain the proper functioning of society. Biometrics is the science that measures and analyzes the physical or behavioral characteristics of a person for identification purposes [23]. According to Jain and Kumar (2012), in order to achieve an appropriate authentication, body traits must satisfy two fundamental premises: to be unique for each individual (distinctiveness) and not to change over time (permanence) [13]. Among several biometric traits such as the face, fingerprints, palm prints, hand geometry, and voice, the human iris is one of the most accurate biometrics [2,8,18], since an iris authentication process has stability, speed, uniqueness and reliability for individual verification [20].

Supported by Consejo Nacional de Ciencia y Tecnología, CONACYT, Mexico.

C. Brito-Loeza et al. (Eds.): ISICS 2022, CCIS 1569, pp. 44–56, 2022.
https://doi.org/10.1007/978-3-030-98457-1_4

The iris is the colored annular ring that surrounds the pupil. The pattern formation that makes it unique is developed in the first year of life [19]. This complex pattern randomly formed in the iris is a physical trait that can be used to identify individuals uniquely, but this is not a trivial task. As a result, the use of computational methods, especially machine learning techniques, has become necessary to automate a reliable identification process.

In general, the iris recognition process can be separated into four basic stages: image acquisition, pre-processing, feature extraction, and recognition [25]. The image acquisition stage obtains iris images from the subject using cameras and sensors with sufficient quality for accurate recognition. The pre-processing stage involves pupil and iris boundary detection, eyelid removal, and normalization. The feature extraction identifies the most remarkable features for recognition. The recognition stage compares extracted features with stored patterns to give a final result.

The first automatic system for iris recognition was developed by John Daugman, using an efficient integro-differential operator for iris localization, a two-dimensional (2D) Gabor filter for feature extraction, and the Hamming distance for the recognition stage [7,9]. In 1997, Wildes proposed the use of the first derivative of image intensity and Hough transform for iris segmentation, a Laplacian of Gaussian filter to represent iris texture, and normalized correlation for recognition [26]. In 2003, Masek used the circular Hough transform and Canny edge detector to find iris boundaries, Log-Gabor wavelets for feature extraction, and the Hamming distance for recognition [19], similar to Daugman's framework. In 2005, Ma et al. used an iris recognition algorithm based on characterizing local variations of image structures [17]. More recently, some authors have applied machine learning algorithms (e.g., neural networks) for iris pattern recognition [1,24]. Since several advances are reflected in a large number of papers, Bowyer et al. [5], and Alkoot [2], have presented valuable reviews of existing work on iris recognition.

All these aforementioned methods require the iris region to be transformed to polar coordinates. Such transformation needs a very accurate segmentation of the iris region to create an iris pattern mapping that is very similar between images of the same eye. Moreover, due to unconstrained nature of iris images, the relative location of iris patterns varies and cannot be easily mapped to the same locations in polar coordinates without some transformation [4]. Therefore, the goal is to extract features invariant to rotation, illumination and partial occlusion caused by eyelids.

Special points, known as keypoint descriptors are invariant to affine transformations and to partial occlusion. A well-known keypoint descriptor for object recognition is the Scale Invariant Feature Transform (SIFT) [16]. Belcher and Du (2009), have proposed a region-based SIFT for performing recognition directly from annular iris images [4]. In [10] a Gabor wavelet is combined with SIFT for feature extraction on noncooperative images for iris recognition. In 2010, a Gabor wavelet is combined with SIFT for feature extraction on non-cooperative images for iris recognition [10], and in 2013, the Fourier transform was applied on each keypoint obtained by SIFT to get feature points for iris recognition [15]. A keypoint descriptor with low computational cost is the Speeded Up Robust Features (SURF) [3]. SURF have been used for extracting unique features from annular iris images, obtaining satisfactory recognition rates [21,22]. In 2015, an iris recognition system was developed based on SURF keypoints extracted from normalized and enhanced images of the iris, providing a 99.5% accuracy [12].

In this work, a method for iris recognition based on supervised learning using matching statistics of SURF is proposed. With the extracted statistical information, a simple, but innovative, feature vector is created and used by a neural network to find the appropriate parameters for determining whether two images correspond to the same iris or not. The main advantage behind the proposed method is the extraction of statistical features that are implicitly invariant to iris texture transformations and fast computational time.

2 Methods

Our iris recognition system consists of the following main modules: pre-processing, feature extraction, and recognition. Our system does not include an image acquisition module that captures iris images in real-time from the subject; instead, we used a publicly available iris image database.

2.1 Iris Image Database

In order to evaluate our method, we have used a publicly available iris image database called CASIA-IrisV3 with three subsets of images (*lamp, interval, twins*) captured in an indoor environment using near-infrared illumination (CASIA iris image database, http://www.cbsr.ia.ac.cn/english/IrisDatabase. asp). Images were collected at different times (at least one-month interval). We have performed our test only on the *interval* subset (CASIA-Iris-Interval), which is well suited for studying the detailed iris texture features. The *interval* subset contains a total of 2,639 images of 249 subjects (both left and right eye) having a resolution of 320 × 280 pixels in grayscale (see Fig. 1).

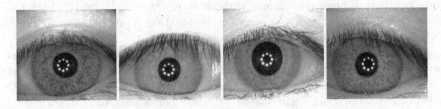

Fig. 1. CASIA iris image database samples.

2.2 Image Pre-processing

The pre-processing module involves localizing the pupil and iris boundaries through the use of the Circular Hough Transform.

Introduced by Duda and Hart [11], the Circular Hough Transform (CHT) is a circle detector working on a binary image, obtained after applying an edge detector to the original image. The Canny edge detector is used to create the contour image I_{edge} [6]. Thus, the contour image is being processed with the Circular Hough Transform H, defined as:

$$H(x_c, y_c, r) = \sum_{j=1}^{n} h(x_j, y_j, x_c, y_c, r) \tag{1}$$

where

$$h(x_j, y_j, x_c, y_c, r) = \begin{cases} 1, \text{ if } (x_j - x_c)^2 + (y_j - y_c)^2 = r^2 \\ 0, \text{ otherwise} \end{cases} \tag{2}$$

and n is the number of pixels detected by the edge detector as a contour.

The h function will take value 1 for each pixel (x_j, y_j) in I_{edge}, that belongs to the circumference defined by the parameters (x_c, y_c, r), where x_c and y_c are the circle center coordinates and r is its radius length.

Since the iris and the pupil are the only two objects with approximately circular shapes inside the original image, the two global maxima of the H function are the suitable choice to segment the iris, defining its inner and outside circular edges (see Fig. 2). Thus, the CHT provides the center of the pupil (x_c, y_c), the inner pupil radius and outer iris radius.

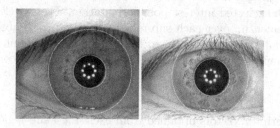

Fig. 2. Pupil and iris boundaries detected by the circular hough transformation.

2.3 Feature Extraction

The feature extraction module constructs a feature vector with efficient characteristics to be used by the recognition module.

For the feature extraction module, the SURF algorithm is used as a local feature detector. This algorithm is applied to a region of interest in the iris of the two images to be compared. Once the SURF points have been obtained, corresponding points between the two images to be compared are computed. Finally, a feature vector is constructed based on statistical metrics obtained from the corresponding points.

SURF Detector. The Speeded Up Robust Features detector is a scale- and rotation-invariant interest point detector and descriptor which achieves high efficiency and robustness [3]. SURF provides a list of interest points (keypoints) and their corresponding descriptors. A SURF detector selects keypoints based on the determinant of the Hessian matrix $\mathcal{H}(\mathbf{x}, \sigma)$ defined in Eq. 3,

$$\mathcal{H}(\mathbf{x}, \sigma) = \begin{bmatrix} L_{xx}(\mathbf{x}, \sigma) & L_{xy}(\mathbf{x}, \sigma) \\ L_{xy}(\mathbf{x}, \sigma) & L_{yy}(\mathbf{x}, \sigma) \end{bmatrix} \tag{3}$$

where $\mathbf{x} = (x, y)$ is a point of an image I, σ is a scaling factor, and $L_{xx}(\mathbf{x}, \sigma)$ represents the convolution of the Gaussian second-order derivative in x-direction with the input image in point $\mathbf{x}$ at scale σ. The determinant of the Hessian matrix $\det(\mathcal{H})$ is equal to the product of its eigenvalues. So, the determinant can be used to locate local maxima and minima in an image (see Eq. 4).

$$\det(\mathcal{H}) = L_{xx}L_{yy} - L_{xy}^2 \tag{4}$$

To guarantee scale invariance, SURF computes Hessian determinant values for every image pixel over scales using box filters of different sizes, producing a determinant pyramid for the entire image. Then, in a $3 \times 3 \times 3$ neighborhood, a non-maximum suppression is applied to localize interest points in the image and over scales.

The SURF descriptor, which characterizes every point of interest, is built using a square region centered around the keypoint and rotated according to the keypoint orientation. The region is divided into 4×4 square sub-regions and Haar-wavelet responses are extracted in horizontal d_x and vertical d_y direction in relation to the selected interest point orientation. The wavelet responses d_x and d_y are summed up over each sub-region along with the absolute values of the responses $|d_x|$ and $|d_y|$ in order to bring information about the polarity of the intensity changes. Thus, for each sub-region, a vector is constructed as in Eq. 5:

$$\mathbf{v} = \left(\sum d_x, \sum d_y, \sum |d_x|, \sum |d_y| \right) \tag{5}$$

Finally, descriptor vectors obtained from each 4×4 sub-region are concatenated to form a descriptor vector of dimension 64. This vector is the keypoint descriptor and it is invariant to changes in illumination. To achieve contrast invariance, the descriptor vector has to be transformed into a unit vector.

Keypoint Matching. Once all points of interest have been detected in the two images to be compared (e.g. Images 1 and 2), the nearest neighbor ratio matching approach is performed to find keypoints correspondence [16]. Thus, an interest point in Image 1 is compared to all interest points in Image 2 by calculating the Euclidean distance between their descriptor vectors. The nearest neighbor in Image 2 to keypoint in Image 1 will be the keypoint with minimum Euclidean distance. A matching pair is detected, only if the distance from the nearest neighbor descriptor is less than γ times the distance from the second nearest neighbor descriptor.

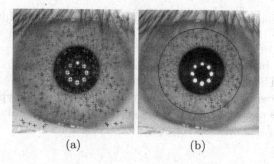

(a)   (b)

Fig. 3. Region of interest to avoid occlusions: a) SURF keypoints from whole image, b) SURF keypoints inside region of interest.

Region of Interest (ROI). Due to changes in illumination, the pupil may contract or expand, causing variations in the region between pupillary and iris boundaries. Such variance can be overcome through normalization, which deals with compensation for elastic deformations in the iris texture. Traditional iris normalization methods transform the iris ring into a rectangular block of a fixed size. Nevertheless, the normalized iris texture may present occlusions from the eyelashes and eyelids. In an average eye, the upper eyelid occludes approximately half the upper iris circle, and the lower eyelid covers one-fourth of the lower iris circle. The left and right portions of the iris are not occluded [21]. In order to avoid such occlusions, we propose to analyze only a region of interest (ROI) inside the iris, which consists of the inner half of the iris circular region, preserving the iris relevant features. Thus, after applying the SURF algorithm to both images entirely, and running the keypoint matching process, all points of interest that are localized outside the ROI will be discarded (see Fig. 3).

Feature Vector. Once all valid keypoints and matching pairs have been obtained, a feature vector is constructed based on matching data between the two images to be compared. Such vector consists of four elements containing statistical data from the keypoint matching process, including ratios of matching pairs, duplicate matches and average localization of keypoints in matching pairs.

In order to calculate the first two elements of the feature vector, we define P_1 as the number of all keypoints detected in the ROI of the source image (e.g. Image 1) and M_{P_1} as the number of keypoints in the ROI of Image 1 that found a corresponding keypoint in the ROI of the target image (e.g. Image 2). With these values, we calculate the ratio of matching pairs R_{M_1} in Image 1, as follows (see Eq. (6)):

$$R_{M_1} = M_{P_1}/P_1 \qquad (6)$$

Similarly, for Image 2, we calculate the ratio of matching pairs R_{M_2} as follows (see Eq. (7)):

$$R_{M_2} = M_{P_2}/P_2 \qquad (7)$$

where P_2 is the number of all keypoints detected in the ROI of Image 2, and M_{P_2} is the number of keypoints in the ROI of Image 2 that found a corresponding keypoint in the ROI of Image 1.

Next, let M be defined as the number of all matching pairs found between Image 1 and 2. Thus, we can obtain the number of duplicate matches in Image 2, this is, the number of keypoints in Image 1 that matched a keypoint in Image 2 that already has one matching pair assigned. The number of duplicate matches D is calculated as follows (see Eq. (8)):

$$D = M - M_{P_2} \tag{8}$$

With these values, we calculate the third element of the feature vector, which is the ratio of duplicate matches R_D in the target image (see Eq. (9)):

$$R_D = D/M \tag{9}$$

In order to include information about the spatial location of keypoints in a matching pair, the mean polar distance between matching points is obtained. Let (r_1, θ_1) and (r_2, θ_2) be the polar coordinates of the two points in a matching pair. Thus, the radial distance d between these points is given by (see Eq. (10)):

$$d = \sqrt{r_1^2 + r_2^2 - 2r_1 r_2 \cos(\theta_2 - \theta_1)} \tag{10}$$

So, the fourth element, the mean polar distance M_{PD} of keypoints in matching pairs, is the following (see Eq. (11)):

$$M_{PD} = \frac{1}{M} \sum_{i=1}^{M} d_i \tag{11}$$

Finally, the feature vector f is constructed as follows (Eq. (12)):

$$f = [R_{M_1}, \ R_{M_2}, \ R_D, \ M_{PD}] \tag{12}$$

2.4   Recognition

For the recognition module, the supervised learning algorithm called neural networks (NN) was used. The classification must determine if a pair of iris images belongs to the same eye (positive samples) or to different eyes (negative samples). Finally, in the case of samples classified as negative, a matching pair verification process based on the keypoints' localization is applied to eliminate false negatives.

Neural Networks. Neural networks are a model that can be used for regression and classification problems. Neural networks are organized into layers: the first layer (input layer) receives the sample feeding the model; the last layer (output layer) delivers the result of the model; the intermediate layers (hidden layers) generate partial results. Each layer contains a number of cells (nodes): in the input layer, the number of nodes is the same as the size of the input vector; in the output layer, the number of nodes is the same as the size of the output or response vector; finally, the number of nodes in the hidden layers is designated experimentally.

Matching Pairs Localization Verification. As we can expect, a negative sample may have none or a small number of keypoints correspondences, where all of them are false matches. In a few cases, a positive sample can have a small number of keypoints correspondences too, but the majority should be valid matches. So, in order to eliminate false negatives, a matching pair verification process is proposed. This process is as follows: once the learning algorithm has classified a pair of images as a negative sample, the polar distance between every two keypoints forming a matching pair in that sample is compared. If the distance's difference is above a threshold (experimentally determined) that matching pair will be considered invalid. At the end, if the majority (above 80%) are valid matching pairs following this verification process, then, that sample will be reclassified as a positive sample; otherwise, it will remain being a negative sample.

Cross Validation. A k-fold cross validation (CV) is performed in order to assess the repeatability on new data. The k-fold CV is carried out as follows: the training set of samples is partitioned into k non-overlapping subsets of (roughly) the same size. A single subset of the k subsets is retained for testing, and the remaining $k - 1$ subsets are used for training. This process is repeated k times (k folds), such that each subset is treated once as the test set. The k results from the folds can then be averaged to form the k-fold CV error rate.

3   Results

3.1   Training and Test Set

Since perfect segmentation success rates were not attained, a subset of the CASIA iris image database was selected to form pairs of images successfully segmented. Each pair simulates the fact of having a model image and a target image. In this data set, every pair with images taken from the same eye was labeled as class 1 and pairs with images taken from different eyes were labeled as class 0. The resulting data set equals the one from Masek's work [7], containing 194,378 pairs of images properly identified with a class, and arranged in random order, where the number of positive samples (class 1) was 1,679, and the number of negative samples (class 0) was 192,699. Out of this data set, 90% of samples was assigned to the training set, and the remaining 10% was assigned to the test set, while keeping the same ratios in the number of positive and negative samples in both databases.

3.2 Experimental Results

To evaluate the performance of our proposed approach, a 10-fold cross-validation method was applied. Our neural network used one hidden layer with 10 nodes, where each node used the sigmoid function as activation function. The input layer comprised four nodes. The output layer contained only one node, whose output value is obtained using a threshold of 0.5, that is, values below or equal 0.5 become zero, values greater than 0.5 become one. This is the method commonly used to make values of the output layer discrete. The standard backpropagation algorithm was used to train our model.

We compared our method with some state-of-the-art iris recognition algorithms tested on the same database in order to evaluate the efficiency of our proposal. The Table 1 shows efficiency results (in percentage) of the average recognition of a 10-fold cross validation. The recognition rate or accuracy is measured by taking the average of FAR and FRR from 100%. Our system obtained a recognition rate of 99.94%, with a False Acceptance Rate (FAR) of 0.00%, and a False Rejection Rate (FRR) of 0.12%. The Receiver Operating Characteristic (ROC) curve shows the accuracy performance of our biometric system based on the relationship of $1-\text{FRR}$ and FAR (see Fig. 4a). A common error measure in biometric systems is the equal error rate (EER) which indicates the error rate where the FAR curve and the FRR curve are equal. The EER of our system is found from those curves as seen in Fig. 4b. During test procedure, we measured the average classification computational time for one pair of images, which includes pre-processing and recognition steps.

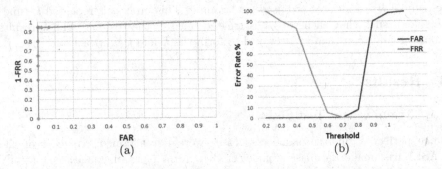

Fig. 4. Performance results of our method: a) the receiver operating characteristic (ROC) curve, and b) the FRR and FAR curves.

According to the results in Table 1, it can be seen that our method has the highest accuracy rate due to invariance to the rotation and translation ensured by SURF encoded in the matching statistics features. Also, the Equal Error Rate (EER) of our system achieved the lowest value of 0.11% compared to other systems. A remarkable result is that our method is entirely error-free for false positive samples, so the system will never fail to recognize a pair of images

Table 1. Comparison of recognition performance for CASIA-IrisV3.

Method	Recognition rate (%)	Equal error rate (%)	Average processing time (s)
Proposed	99.94	0.11	1.18
Masek [19]	99.88	0.23	13.96
Jin et al. [14]	99.62	0.42	2.55
Ma et al. [17]	99.60	0.29	6.91
Ismail et al. [12]	99.50	0.38	1.53
Kumar et al. [15]	98.99	0.40	2.48

corresponding to different eyes. In terms of processing time, our system is the fastest one with an average processing time of 1.18 s, compared to other verification systems; this is due to the fast keypoints extraction process, and a region of interest assuring a minimum number of keypoints, which leads to a faster recognition process.

To analyze the effectiveness of the feature vector proposed, we want to discuss its elements and their corresponding contribution for recognition.

If we analyze some samples of images after obtaining the keypoints matching pairs, we can observe that, in average, if the two images to be compared belong to the same eye, the number of valid matching pairs is greater than the number of valid matching pairs in two images from different eyes (see Fig. 5). This suggests that the first two elements in the feature vector (i.e., ratios of matching) provide a practical threshold to classify positive and negative samples. In a few cases (see Fig. 6a), where positive samples show a small matching ratio (i.e., fewer matching pairs found), these two features alone are not enough to avoid false negatives. Regarding this, we observed that a negative sample presents not only a few, but also wrong matching pairs, e.g., duplicate matches (see Fig. 6b) and a general mismatch of keypoints location in matching pairs (see Fig. 5b). So, in order to correctly distinguish negative samples, the ratio of duplicate matches and the average polar distance, were taken as features. This last feature, considers the

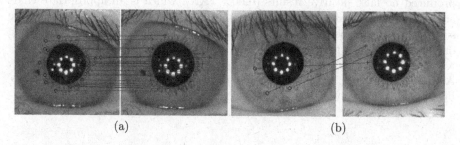

       (a)   (b)

Fig. 5. Keypoint matching samples inside the ROI: a) images from the same eye, b) images from different eyes.

average location of all keypoints in matching pairs; expecting that the worse the mismatch of corresponding keypoints location the larger the average polar distance may be.

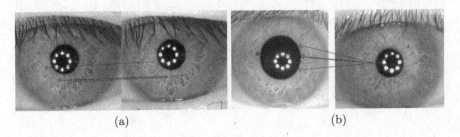

(a)   (b)

Fig. 6. Cases: a) positive sample with a small matching ratio, b) negative sample with duplicate matches.

The region of interest (ROI) is practical and acceptable for accurate iris recognition, considering that the detailed texture of the iris remains unaltered, although it stretches and contracts to adjust the pupil's size in response to light [2]. Reliability of the matching pairs localization is achieved, since polar coordinates are computed based on a normalized iris radio between 0 (pupil's ending contour) and 1 (iris' ending contour).

4   Conclusions

In this paper, we have presented an efficient method for iris recognition based on SURF matching statistics to generate a novel feature vector showing a recognition rate of 99.94%. This method uses supervised learning to classify whether a pair of iris images belongs to the same eye or different eyes. It exploits the main iris features within a practical region of interest to avoid upper and lower eyelid occlusion. Experimental results on CASIA-IrisV3 have illustrated the encouraging performance of the proposed method. In particular, the recognition system produced no false positive results (0.00% FAR), which is an appropriate characteristic that should be present in biometric security systems. A comparative study between our method and other existing methods has been performed being our method the one presenting the best recognition results.

Acknowledgements. CASIA-IrisV3 was used from the Chinese Academy of Sciences' Institute of Automation.

References

1. Abiyev, R., Altunkaya, K.: Personal Iris recognition using neural networks. IJSIA **2**(2), 41–50 (2008)
2. Alkoot, F.M.: A review on advances in iris recognition methods. Int. J. Comput. Eng. Res. **3**(1), 1–9 (2012)
3. Bay, H., Tuytelaars, T., Van Gool, L.: SURF: speeded up robust features. In: Leonardis, A., Bischof, H., Pinz, A. (eds.) ECCV 2006. LNCS, vol. 3951, pp. 404–417. Springer, Heidelberg (2006). https://doi.org/10.1007/11744023_32
4. Belcher, C., Du, Y.: Region-based SIFT approach to iris recognition. Opt. Lasers Eng. **47**(1), 139–147 (2009)
5. Bowyer, K.W., Hollingsworth, K.P., Flynn, P.J.: A survey of iris biometrics research: 2008–2010. In: Burge, M., Bowyer, K. (eds.) Handbook of Iris Recognition. Advances in Computer Vision and Pattern Recognition. Springer, London (2013). https://doi.org/10.1007/978-1-4471-4402-1_2
6. Canny, J.: A computational approach to edge detection. IEEE T. Pattern Anal. PAMI **8**(6), 679–698 (1986)
7. Daugman, J.G.: Biometric personal identification system based on Iris analysis. US Patent 5,291,560 (1994)
8. Daugman, J.G.: How Iris recognition works. IEEE Trans. Circ. Syst. Video Technol. **14**(1), 21–30 (2004)
9. Daugman, J.G.: Probing the uniqueness and randomness of IrisCodes: results from 200 Billion Iris pair comparisons. Proc. IEEE **94**(11), 1927–1935 (2006)
10. Du, Y., Belcher, C., Zhou, Z.: Scale invariant Gabor descriptor-based noncooperative Iris recognition. EURASIP J. Adv. Sig. Process. **2010**(1), 1–13 (2010). https://doi.org/10.1155/2010/936512
11. Duda, R.O., Hart, P.E.: Use of the Hough transformation to detect lines and curves in pictures. Commun. ACM **15**(1), 11–15 (1972)
12. Ismail, A.I., Ali, H.S., Farag, F.A.: Efficient enhancement and matching for iris recognition using SURF. In: National Symposium on Information Technology: Towards New Smart World (NSITNSW), pp. 1–5. IEEE (2015)
13. Jain, A.K., Kumar, A.: Biometric recognition: an overview. In: Mordini, E., Tzovaras, D. (eds.) Second Generation Biometrics: The Ethical, Legal and Social Context. The International Library of Ethics, Law and Technology. Springer, Dordrecht (2012). https://doi.org/10.1007/978-94-007-3892-8_3
14. Jin, Q., Tong, X., Ma, P., Bo, S.: Iris recognition by new local invariant feature descriptor. J. Comput. Inf. Syst. **9**(5), 1943–1948 (2013)
15. Kumar, A., Majhi, B.: Isometric efficient and accurate Fourier-SIFT method in Iris recognition system. In: International Conference on Communications and Signal Processing (ICCSP), pp. 809–813. IEEE (2013)
16. Lowe, D.G.: Distinctive image features from scale-invariant keypoints. Int. J. Comput. Vis. **60**(2), 91–110 (2004). https://doi.org/10.1023/B:VISI.0000029664.99615.94
17. Ma, L., Tan, T., Wang, Y., Zhang, D.: Local intensity variation analysis for iris recognition. Pattern Recogn. **37**(6), 1287–1298 (2004)
18. Malgheet, J.R., Manshor, N.B., Affendey, L.S.: Iris recognition development techniques: a comprehensive review. Complexity **2021**, 1–32 (2021)
19. Masek, L.: Recognition of Human Iris Patterns for Biometric Identification. The University of Western Australia, School of Computer Science and Software Engineering (2003)

20. Mehrotra, H., Badrinath, G.S., Majhi, B., Gupta, P.: An efficient dual stage approach for Iris feature extraction using interest point pairing. In: IEEE Workshop on Computational Intelligence in Biometrics: Theory, Algorithms, and Applications, pp. 59–62. IEEE (2009)
21. Mehrotra, H., Majhi, B., Gupta, P.: Annular Iris recognition using SURF. In: Chaudhury, S., Mitra, S., Murthy, C.A., Sastry, P.S., Pal, S.K. (eds.) PReMI 2009. LNCS, vol. 5909, pp. 464–469. Springer, Heidelberg (2009). https://doi.org/10.1007/978-3-642-11164-8_75
22. Mehrotra, H., Sa, P.K., Majhi, B.: Fast segmentation and adaptive surf descriptor for iris recognition. Math. Comput. Model. 58(1–2), 132–146 (2013)
23. Ross, A.: Iris recognition: the path forward. Computer 43(2), 30–35 (2010)
24. Saminathan, K., Chithra Devi, M., Chakravarthy, T.: Pair of Iris recognition for personal identification using artificial neural networks. IJCSI 9(1), 324–327 (2012)
25. Sheela, S.V., Vijaya, P.A.: Iris recognition methods - survey. Int. J. Comput. Appl. 3(5), 19–25 (2010)
26. Wildes, R.P.: Iris recognition: an emerging biometric technology. Proc. IEEE 85(9), 1348–1363 (1997)

Convolutional Neural Network for Segmentation of Single Cell Gel Electrophoresis Assay

Daniel Ruz-Suarez[1]([✉])(iD), Anabel Martin-Gonzalez[1](iD), Carlos Brito-Loeza[1](iD), and Elda Leonor Pacheco-Pantoja[2](iD)

[1] Computational Learning and Imaging Research, Facultad de Matemáticas, Universidad Autónoma de Yucatán, Merida 97115, Mexico
danielruzsuarez@gmail.com, {amarting,carlos.brito}@correo.uady.mx
[2] Mexico Medicine School, Health Sciences Division, Universidad Anáhuac Mayab, Km 15.5 Carr. Mérida-Progreso, Mérida, Yucatán, Mexico
elda.pacheco@anahuac.mx

Abstract. The single cell gel electrophoresis assay, which is also referred to as the comet assay, is a quantitative method by which visual evidence of DNA damage in individual cells may be measured. Since this assay is sensitive and simple to perform, it is widely used in several areas including human biomonitoring, genotoxicology, and ecological monitoring. In the last decades, various computer systems have implemented segmentation algorithms based on traditional threshold techniques rather than efficient deep learning methods to automatically identify cells in comet assay output images. This paper presents a fully convolutional neural network based system, named U-NetComet, to automate comets segmentation, minimizing user interaction and providing reproducible measurements. A comparison of our method with a commercial system has been performed, and results showed that our system is more efficient and reliable.

Keywords: Comet assay · Single cell gel · Segmentation · Convolutional neural network · Deep learning

1 Introduction

Human body cells are constantly exposed to harmful agents that deteriorate DNA. The comet or single cell gel electrophoresis (SCGE) assay is a versatile technique, introduced by Ostling and Johanson (1984), to detect DNA damage at the level of single cells for use in biological research [9]. In this method, DNA electrophoresis is performed, and a fluorescent dye is used for staining of the DNA [2]. The resultant image obtained with this technique is similar to a comet, in which the head consists of undamaged DNA, and the tail encloses broken pieces of DNA (see Fig. 1). The amount of DNA fragments migrating out of the cell nucleus during electrophoresis is related to the extent of DNA damage.

© Springer Nature Switzerland AG 2022
C. Brito-Loeza et al. (Eds.): ISICS 2022, CCIS 1569, pp. 57–68, 2022.
https://doi.org/10.1007/978-3-030-98457-1_5

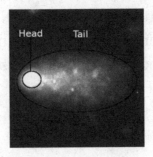

Fig. 1. Comet assay cell image

Most methods for analyzing comet assay images use thresholding-based methods; such is the case of Helma and Uhl (2000), and Końca et al. (2003) whose algorithms define a threshold value, depending on a maximum brightness pixel value, to segment comets and to define their heads [6,7]. Gyori et al. (2014) developed a free software tool, known as OpenComet, that automatically segments comets by adaptive thresholding and detects their heads using an intensity profile analysis [4]. In 2018, Lee et al., proposed a more sophisticated system, named HiComet [8], which finds the segmentation threshold value automatically with minimum user intervention, including partitioning of overlapped comets. However, these methods have to define features manually, making the system less robust when processing comets with noisy backgrounds or overlapped. Other methods have been proposed to classify the DNA damage in comet assay images [1,5].

In the last decade, deep learning methods have shown their outstanding performance for segmentation tasks [11], learning better features to identify objects. Therefore, in this paper, we proposed a fully-automated segmentation system, based on a convolutional neural network, to process SCGE assay images, extracting essential features to efficiently determine head and tail of comets.

2   Methodology

2.1   System Overview

The proposed imaging system, named U-NetComet, for identification and extraction of comet assay cells is composed of a series of modules that work together to generate the outputs (see Fig. 2). The system's input is an image in grayscale or RGB format. The segmentation module determines whether a pixel belongs to the head or tail of a comet, or background. Next, the system identifies overlaid comets. Then, comet contours are defined and parametric features are extracted. Finally, the system's two outputs are: the original input image with additional contours, indicating the region of the comet and its head; and a CSV file with all the parametric data automatically extracted from the comets.

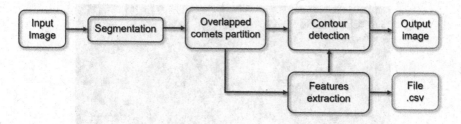

Fig. 2. U-NetComet system diagram

2.2 Image Database

The original dataset consists of 140 comet assay images, in grayscale format, with resolution of 1388 × 1038 pixels, containing cells with different degrees of damage, various shapes and sizes due to magnifying lens (see Fig. 3(a)). In order to form a training and validation set, 130 images were randomly selected, whereas, the remaining 10 images completed the test set.

In order to avoid training issues due to low memory and excessive processing time, the 130 images were cropped into smaller images of 288×288 pixels. The number of images extracted from each original image varied depending on the number of comets they contained (see Fig. 3(b–c)). A total of 751 images were created and divided into a training set (664 images), and a validation set (87 images). In the testing phase, we adopted the overlap-tile strategy described in [11] to evaluate the performance of the model. The ground truth from all images in the database was manually generated.

2.3 Segmentation

The first step in the system is to classify pixels in the input image into one of three classes: background (class 0), tail (class 1), and head (class 2). This process is performed by the convolutional neural network, U-Net [11]. Our segmentation module is developed for analyzing grayscale (one channel) images, thus, RGB formats (three channels) are transformed into grayscale format. In case the input image has a resolution larger than 288 × 288 (training images dimension), we used the overlap-tile strategy; thus, the system can process images from the test set (1388 × 1038), taking into consideration that segmentation time would be longer.

At the end, the output of this module is a map with a three channels depth (one channel per class), consisting of probabilities belonging to each class. Out of this map, the system finds the channel number that has the highest probability for each pixel. As a result, a segmented image is obtained, where each pixel has assigned a value of 0, 1 or 2.

The U-Net network is made up of two parts, the first one is called encoder, where dimensions of activation maps decrease on each layer, and the second part is called decoder, in which dimensions of activation maps increase layer by

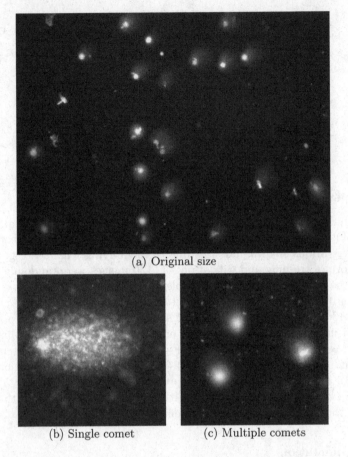

(a) Original size

(b) Single comet   (c) Multiple comets

Fig. 3. Comet assay dataset samples: original size and cropped images.

layer until reaching the dimensions of input image. We applied zero-padding to fill out with zeros the edge limits of the activation maps, so that, after each convolution, the size of every activation map remains the same. The complete U-Net architecture is shown in Table 1.

The U-Net model was trained with parameters randomly initialized by the Glorot uniform initialization, also called Xavier uniform initialization [3]. The loss function used was the categorical Cross-Entropy, the learning rate was set to 1×10^{-4}, and the Adam optimizer was adopted. The training process was carried out for 50 epochs. To avoid overfitting, we used the hold-out validation method; therefore, the model weights were saved only when the loss value in the validation set decreased in any of the 50 training cycles; in other words, we saved the model weights when the "sweet spot" was reached.

The test set to evaluate our U-NetComet system consisted of 10 images manually segmented. The metric adopted to examine segmentation performance of the system was the F1-score (similar to Dice Coefficient), including its precision and recall:

Table 1. U-Net architecture

	Level	Layer	Filter	Activation	Output size
Input					$288 \times 288 \times 1$
Encoder	Level 1	Convolution 1	$3 \times 3/64$	ReLU	$288 \times 288 \times 64$
		Convolution 2	$3 \times 3/64$	ReLU	$288 \times 288 \times 64$
		Maxpooling			$144 \times 144 \times 64$
	Level 2	Convolution 3	$3 \times 3/128$	ReLU	$144 \times 144 \times 128$
		Convolution 4	$3 \times 3/128$	ReLU	$144 \times 144 \times 128$
		Maxpooling			$72 \times 72 \times 128$
	Level 3	Convolution 5	$3 \times 3/256$	ReLU	$72 \times 72 \times 256$
		Convolution 6	$3 \times 3/256$	ReLU	$72 \times 72 \times 256$
		Maxpooling			$36 \times 36 \times 256$
	Level 4	Convolution 7	$3 \times 3/512$	ReLU	$36 \times 36 \times 512$
		Convolution 8	$3 \times 3/512$	ReLU	$36 \times 36 \times 512$
		Maxpooling			$18 \times 18 \times 512$
Bridge	Level 5	Convolution 9	$3 \times 3/1024$	ReLU	$18 \times 18 \times 1024$
		Convolution 10	$3 \times 3/1024$	ReLU	$18 \times 18 \times 1024$
Decoder	Level 6	Up-Convolution	$2 \times 2/512$	ReLU	$36 \times 36 \times 512$
		Concatenation with Conv 8			$36 \times 36 \times 1024$
		Convolution 11	$3 \times 3/512$	ReLU	$36 \times 36 \times 512$
		Convolution 12	$3 \times 3/512$	ReLU	$36 \times 36 \times 512$
	Level 7	Up-Convolution	$2 \times 2/256$	ReLU	$72 \times 72 \times 256$
		Concatenation with Conv 6			$72 \times 72 \times 512$
		Convolution 13	$3 \times 3/256$	ReLU	$72 \times 72 \times 256$
		Convolution 14	$3 \times 3/256$	ReLU	$72 \times 72 \times 256$
	Level 8	Up-Convolution	$2 \times 2/256$	ReLU	$144 \times 144 \times 128$
		Concatenation with Conv 4			$144 \times 144 \times 256$
		Convolution 15	$3 \times 3/128$	ReLU	$144 \times 144 \times 128$
		Convolution 16	$3 \times 3/128$	ReLU	$144 \times 144 \times 128$
	Level 9	Up-Convolution	$2 \times 2/64$	ReLU	$288 \times 288 \times 64$
		Concatenation withConv 2			$288 \times 288 \times 128$
		Convolution 17	$3 \times 3/64$	ReLU	$288 \times 288 \times 64$
		Convolution 18	$3 \times 3/64$	ReLU	$288 \times 288 \times 64$
Output		Convolution 19	$3 \times 3/3$	Softmax	$288 \times 288 \times 3$

$$Precision = \frac{TP}{TP + FP}$$

$$Recall = \frac{TP}{TP + FN}$$

Thus, the F1-score is defined as:

$$F1 = \frac{2 \cdot Precision \cdot Recall}{Precision + Recall}$$

The true positive (TP), false positive (FP), true negative (TN), and false negative (FN) values are used to calculate these metrics. However, as the segmentation is multiclass (three classes), in order to calculate the metrics in a binary way, a true value corresponds to a pixel of the class that is being evaluated and a false value corresponds to a pixel of the two classes remaining. For example, when evaluating the precision or recall of the tail class, the true value is a tail pixel and the false value is a head or background pixel.

2.4 Overlapped Comets Partition

This process performs the task of finding the approximate limits of superimposed comets, partitioning overlapped comets into individual comets. For this purpose, we use the watershed algorithm [10], which consists of determining the areas close to a marker or maximum, according to a distance map. Then, the system identifies the regions that have two or more heads as overlapping comets. Such heads are used as markers for the watershed algorithm, and the grayscale image is used as the distance map.

2.5 Feature Extraction

At this point in the system process, we already have the segmented image, as well as the overlapping comet regions partitioned, so now, the system is able to extract, from each comet, the characteristics of interest defined in Table 2.

Table 2. Comet features extracted by U-NetComet

Features	Definition
Comet area	Number of pixels in the comet
Comet length	Distance from where the comet starts to where it ends
Comet DNA content	Sum of the intensities of comet pixels
Comet average intensity	Comet DNA content divided by comet area
Head area	Number of pixels in the head
Head diameter	Distance from where the head starts to where it ends
Head DNA content	Sum of the intensities of the head pixels
Head average intensity	Head DNA content divided by head area
Head DNA%	Percentage of head DNA content with respect to the comet DNA content
Tail area	Number of pixels in the tail
Tail length	Distance from where the tail starts to where it ends
Tail DNA content	Sum of the intensities of the tail pixels
Tail average intensity	Tail DNA content divided by tail area
Tail DNA%	Percentage of tail DNA content with respect to the comet DNA content
Tail moment	Product between the length of the comet and the tail DNA%
Olive moment	Product of the tail DNA% with the distance between the centroids of the head and tail

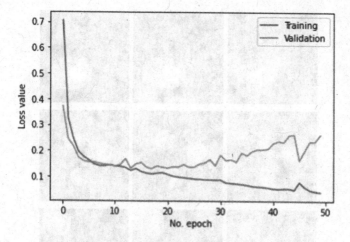

Fig. 4. Deep model learning curves

These numerical features are saved in a CSV file, and serve for further DNA cells damage analysis done by experts.

2.6 Contour Detection

This module takes the segmented image to find the contours of the regions marked as comets, as well as the contours of the regions marked as heads, by means of a mathematical morphology algorithm, which searches for connected regions. These contours are colored blue for non-overlapping comets and gray for overlapping comets. The head's contour is colored in red.

3 Results

Training and validation learning curves from the U-Net model are shown in Fig. 4. As seen in the graph, the loss value for the validation set was increasing after 20 epochs, indicating a model overfitting during the training process. However, with the hold-out validation method included, we saved the model weights with the minimum loss value, ensuring the best segmentation model all over the learning process.

Qualitative segmentation outputs performed by the U-Net model during validation are shown in Fig. 5. As we can observe, pixels from overlapped comets are classified correctly, but still not identified as belonging to different comets. A sample showing the partition of two overlapping comets is illustrated in Fig. 6.

Comparison experiments were done versus the state-of-the-art system, named OpenComet.In order to compare segmentation of both systems, the OpenComet output images were processed manually to generate its corresponding segmented images. Segmentation results, from both algorithms, obtained using the test set, are shown in Table 3. Figures 7, 8 and 9 show samples of both systems' outputs.

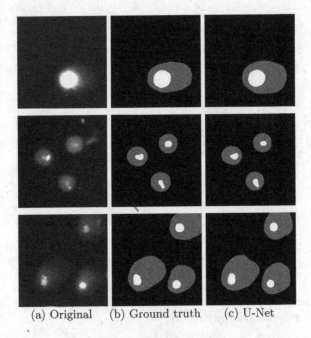

(a) Original   (b) Ground truth   (c) U-Net

Fig. 5. U-Net validation segmentation samples

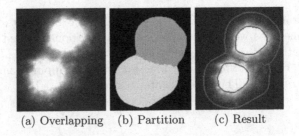

(a) Overlapping   (b) Partition   (c) Result

Fig. 6. Overlapped comet partition process

Table 3. Segmentation results: U-NetComet vs OpenComet

	U-NetComet			OpenComet		
	Precision	Recall	F1 score	Precision	Recall	F1 score
Background	0.974	0.969	**0.972**	0.888	0.992	0.937
Tail	0.812	0.850	**0.831**	0.871	0.206	0.333
Head	0.867	0.694	**0.771**	0.208	0.447	0.284
Average	0.884	0.838	**0.858**	0.656	0.548	0.518

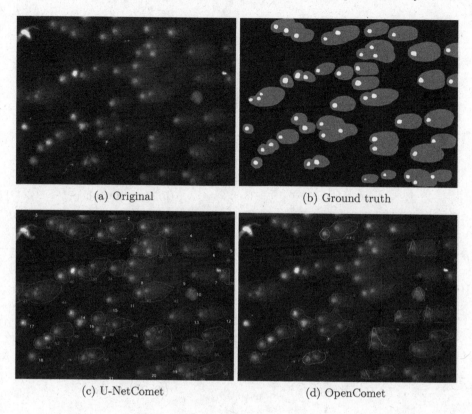

(a) Original   (b) Ground truth

(c) U-NetComet   (d) OpenComet

Fig. 7. Results from test image 1

4   Discussion

Analyzing metrics in Table 3, we can highlight the following.

The recall metric indicates that 85% of the pixels marked as tail in the ground truth (manually segmented images) were classified as tail, and the precision indicates that from all the pixels marked as tail, only 81.2% belongs to that class. This suggests that some of the manually segmented comets were not identified by the U-NetComet system.

Regarding the head class, only 69.4% of pixels marked as head in the ground truth were correctly classified, and 86.7% of all pixels marked as head belongs to this class. This indicates that the system has a significant high precision on classifying a pixel as head.

Based on the F1-score metric, the U-NetComet obtained without doubt much better segmentation results than the OpenComet.

Figure 7 shows an image of the comet assay with a large number of cells, most of which are overlapping. While OpenComet does not segment most of the comets contained in the image, U-NetComet segments most of them. Furthermore, U-NetComet is capable of segmenting the size of heads closer to the ground truth

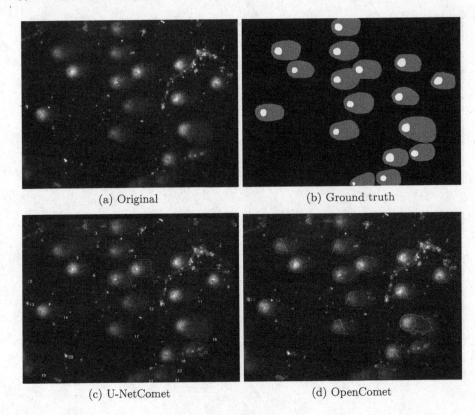

(a) Original   (b) Ground truth

(c) U-NetComet   (d) OpenComet

Fig. 8. Results from test image 2

than OpenComet. The bad point of the proposed system in this figure is the overlapping comet partition, since some divisions are incorrect, such as comets 33 and 35.

In Fig. 8, the U-NetComet system segments the head size better than the OpenComet system, however, it's not very similar to the ground truth. Additionally, the U-NetComet segmentation of comet 26 is better than OpenComet, because U-NetComet ignores the noise that does not belong to the comet.

In Fig. 9, U-NetComet segments most of the comets contained in the image, while OpenComet ignores some comets located on the right side. Again, head segmentation is better on U-NetComet. Regarding the overlapping comet partitioning, incorrect partitions are observed, such as cometas 36 and 37.

The main contribution of this work is the inclusion of a deep learning model for segmentation of comet assay cells, instead of traditional segmentation techniques, such as thresholding, used in the state-of-the-art methods. Thus, our model implements a more sophisticated feature extracting engine through all the hidden layers, and performing better the task of classifying each pixel contained in the image as a pixel associated to the background, tail or head of a comet.

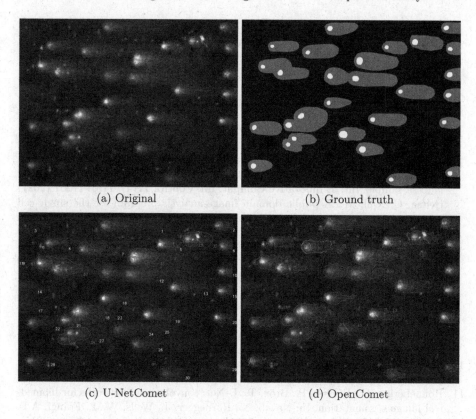

(a) Original   (b) Ground truth

(c) U-NetComet   (d) OpenComet

Fig. 9. Results from test image 3

Finally, we consider this samples' diversity in our dataset is a good component to enhance the learning process of our system, and therefore, increasing the possibility of detecting all types of comets.

5 Conclusion

An imaging system for segmentation of comet assay cells, named U-NetComet, based on a fully-convolutional neural network is proposed. During testing phase, U-NetComet has shown more efficient results than systems based on thresholding techniques, which take less computational processing time, but have lower performance. This developed computer assisted biomedical tool, can pave the path to solve segmentation task in comet assay experiments towards implementation of more complex deep learning models.

References

1. Atila, U., Yusuf Yargı, B., Sehirli, E., Turan, M.K.: Classification of dna damages on segmented comet assay images using convolutional neural network. Comput. Methods Programs Biomed. **186**, 105192 (2020)

2. Fairbairn, D.W., Olive, P.L., O'Neill, K.L.: The comet assay: a comprehensive review. Mutat. Res./Rev. Genet. Toxicol. **339**(1), 37–59 (1995)
3. Glorot, X., Bengio, Y.: Understanding the difficulty of training deep feedforward neural networks. In: Proceedings of the 13th International Conference on Artificial Intelligence and Statistics (AISTATS), pp. 249–256. Sardinia, Italy (2010)
4. Gyori, B.M., Venkatachalam, G., Thiagarajan, P., Hsu, D., Clement, M.V.: OpenComet: an automated tool for comet assay image analysis. Redox Biol. **2**(1), 457–465 (2014)
5. Hafiyan, Y.T., Yanuaryska, R.D., Anarossi, E., Sutanto, V.M., Triyanto, J., Sakakibara, Y.: A hybrid convolutional neural network-extreme learning machine with augmented dataset for DNA damage classification using comet assay from buccal mucosa sample. Int. J. Innovative Comput. Inf. Control **17**(4), 1191–11201 (2021)
6. Helma, C., Uhl, M.: A public domain image-analysis program for the single-cell gel- electrophoresis (comet) assay. Mutat. Res. Genet. Toxicol. Environ. Mutagen. **466**(1), 9–15 (2000)
7. Końca, K., et al.: A cross-platform public domain PC image-analysis program for the comet assay. Mutat. Res. Genet. Toxicol. Environ. Mutagen. **534**(1–2), 15–20 (2003) .
8. Lee, T., et al.: HiComet: a high-throughput comet analysis tool for large-scale DNA damage assessment. BMC Bioinform. **19**(1), 49–61 (2018)
9. Ostling, O., Johanson, K.: Microelectrophoretic study of radiation-induced DNA damages in individual mammalian cells. Biochem. Biophys. Res. Commun. **123**(1), 291–298 (1984)
10. Roerdink, J.B., Meijster, A.: The watershed transform: definitions, algorithms and parallelization strategies. Fund. Inform. **41**(1–2), 187–228 (2000)
11. Ronneberger, O., Fischer, P., Brox, T.: U-Net: convolutional networks for biomedical image segmentation. In: Navab, N., Hornegger, J., Wells, W.M., Frangi, A.F. (eds.) MICCAI 2015. LNCS, vol. 9351, pp. 234–241. Springer, Cham (2015). https://doi.org/10.1007/978-3-319-24574-4_28 Biomedical Image Segmentation. Medical Image Computing and Computer-Assisted Intervention – MICCAI 2015 (2015)

Evaluation of Human SCD Test by Digital Image Analysis

V. Castañeda[1,2,3(✉)], C. A. Figueroa[3], F. Horta[3,4], S. Vargas[1,3], A. García[1,3], J. Jara-Wilde[1], and S. Härtel[1]

[1] Laboratory of Scientific Image Analysis, Institute of Biomedical Sciences, Faculty of Medicine, University of Chile, Santiago, Chile
vcastane@uchile.cl
[2] Medical Technology Department, Faculty of Medicine, University of Chile, Santiago, Chile
[3] Center of Digital Semen Analysis (CEDAI), Santiago, Chile
[4] Education Program in Reproduction and Development, Department of Obstetrics and Gynecology, Monash University, Clayton, VIC 3168, Australia

Abstract. The last decade has shown substantial increasing use of Sperm Chromatin Dispersion tests (SCDt) to evaluate DNA-fragmentation in human sperm. SCDt has been proven advantageous over other techniques. However, the visual evaluation remains a subjective component. The goal of this work was to develop an automated, repeatable and objective image analysis method to evaluate human DNA-fragmentation from SCDt images. SCDt was applied to 12 volunteer male sperm samples imaged by bright-field microscopy. Sperm cell cores (heads) were segmented to extract geometric and texture features. Each sperm cell was manually labeled by experts, in order to build a ground truth (GT) dataset to train a support vector machine for fragmented/non-fragmented DNA classification. The overall predictive performance was assessed using three individual datasets: 100% for training, 10-fold cross-validation, and 70% training/30% testing split. We defined and assessed 11 individual datasets simulating the behavior of the classifier for new, unknown samples. Classification accuracy and incorrectly classified instances show agreement between the proposed method and GT. Results show overall accuracy >90% in the three individual datasets, and a false positive rate <7%. We tested with balanced and imbalanced training datasets (regarding the number of fragmented and non-fragmented sperm cells). Results from the imbalanced dataset show better performance. The predictive performance in the new sample test shows average accuracy >95% and a false positive rate ~2%. Evaluation of the differences between reported DNA-fragmentation percentages against GT show an average/maximum of 4.17%/11.35%, close to the 10% maximum error recommended by the WHO manual for clinical laboratories.

Keywords: Sperm chromatin dispersion test · Sperm DNA fragmentation · Digital image analysis

© Springer Nature Switzerland AG 2022
C. Brito-Loeza et al. (Eds.): ISICS 2022, CCIS 1569, pp. 69–82, 2022.
https://doi.org/10.1007/978-3-030-98457-1_6

1 Introduction

To date, there is abundant evidence of a strong association between sperm DNA fragmentation and male infertility. Specifically, a positive correlation has been observed in sperm cells between DNA fragmentation and altered motility [22, 31, 32], and between DNA fragmentation and morphology [8]. Several studies have evaluated the relationship between results of DNA fragmentation tests and medically assisted reproduction outcomes [3, 4, 22, 29, 31, 32], such as pregnancy rates and higher post implantation spontaneous miscarriage rates [18, 20, 27, 28, 34]. DNA damage has been also associated with several infertility phenotypes, including unexplained infertility, repeated intrauterine and *in vitro* fertilization (IVF) failure, and recurrent miscarriage [5, 7, 23, 24, 26, 30]. These studies suggest that DNA fragmentation may be a key factor in pregnancy failures and should be considered as a high necessity in routine patient care, with more frequency and priority for patients with a history of long-standing infertility or repeated IVF failure [1, 6, 25]. SCDt is widely accepted in the clinical praxis due to its low cost, simple, and fast implementation [9, 12]. For SCDt, fragmented DNA sperm cells fail to produce a characteristic halo of dispersed DNA loops [9]. This halo is typically observed in sperm cells with non-fragmented DNA under treatment for acid denaturation and removal of nuclear proteins. The results of SCDt have been shown to be highly consistent with other analysis techniques of DNA fragmentation, including SCSA and TUNEL [10, 11]. SCDt usage allows a common criterion to be applied among laboratories. However, it relies on visual analysis which lacks objectivity and independence from the observer [2, 19]. Some automated algorithms for segmenting and quantifying DNA fragmentation were found in the literature. Work of Rekha et al. [35] describes a method using K-Means in order to segment images obtaining basic features for posterior separation. Dimitriadis [36] showed a developed system based on smartphone to measure DNA Fragmentation (Halo Sperm), reporting a -10.4% to 11.8% error with an average of 5.7%. There is no description of used method. In this context, we propose an automated image analysis method for the segmentation of human sperm cells and DNA fragmentation classification for accurate, non-biased results.

2 Methodology

Our method comprises three main steps: (i) SCDt image segmentation of sperm cells core (or head) and halo; (ii) feature extraction of the segmented structures, where a feature vector is calculated for every detected sperm cell; and (iii) classification of each sperm cell DNA, according to its feature vector, as fragmented or non-fragmented. A ground truth dataset was created and used to train and validate a supervised learning model for the classification step.

2.1 Segmentation of Sperm Cell Core and Halo

Image processing algorithms were implemented and applied in IDL (Interactive Data Language; Harris Geospatial; Broomfield, CO, USA) upon RGB images. Since typical RGB camera sensors have double the number of green pixels, the algorithms were applied only to the green channel which obtain necessary information for processing. First, the intensity gradient (Sobel filtering) was computed to normalize variable illumination levels. Then, adaptive thresholding based on Otsu and watershed algorithms were applied to produce a segmented binary image for the regions of interest (ROIs) of each sperm cell: core and halo. Watershed is used only to separate segmented sperm cell from distance map of ROIs. Next, morphological operators were applied to filter out ROIs by size, discarding image artifacts such as debris. Finally, having the segmented sperm cell (halo and core), a texture detector based on ISO-Alpha algorithm and thresholding was applied to split core and halo pixels. The axis-aligned bounding boxes for core and halo ROIs were also extracted.

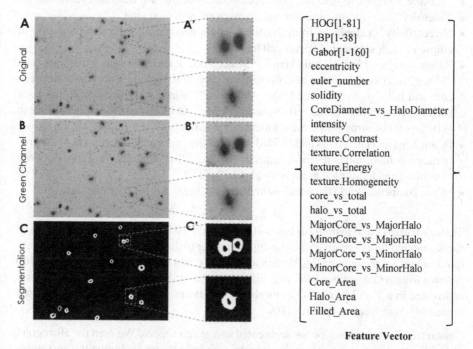

Fig. 1. Left: Image acquisition and Halo segmentation example. A: Bright-field microscopy RGB SCDt image. B: Image green channel. C: Segmented halo areas for each sperm cell. A'-C': Selected zoomed-in regions showing representative sperm cell cores. **Right:** Feature vector used in the classification method composed of morphological, texture and geometrical features.

2.2 Feature Extraction

Several features were extracted from the ROIs in order to evaluate sperm DNA fragmentation. First, a best-fit ellipse is calculated for each segmented sperm cell core, in order to rotate the core towards the orientation of its major axis, and to ensure that all the segmented ROIs are aligned to allow for comparable features. An extra padding area of 25% of the bounding box was defined to incorporate surrounding information for the sperm cells. A total of 298 features were calculated (see Fig. 1). An example of a segmented sperm cell and extracted morphological features is shown in the Fig. 2.

Morphological Features

- "Euler number" for counting ROI holes. Correctly segmented sperm cells have only one hole (the core/head), unlike adjacent sperm cells that appear fused in the image.
- "Solidity" coefficient between filled area (halo and core) and halo area (core only).
- "Intensity" ratio for maximum/mean intensity of each halo area
- "Eccentricity", calculated from the focal length and the minor axis of the best-fit ellipse of each segmented sperm cell halo.
- Ratios between "Major Axis Halo", "Minor Axis Halo", "Major Axis Core" and "Minor Axis Core" from the best-fit ellipse of each ROI, provide aspect ratios between core and halo. Note that the "Major Axis Halo"/"Minor Axis Core" ratio has been used for classifying sperm cells with fragmented DNA (values <1/3, according to [9]), depending strongly on the segmentation quality.
- "Core Area", "Halo Area" and "Filled Area" of the sperm cell correspond to the area of the core, halo, and core+halo, respectively, after filling all holes; the ratios between core/filled and halo/filled areas were also included.
- "Core Diameter/Halo Diameter" ratio from best-fit circles for core and halo.

Texture features and histogram-based statistics were computed in the bounding box of the segmented ROIs (green channel image), in order to discriminate halo and core. Texture features are mean intensity, statistical moments, and entropy. We also included 160 features from a Gabor filter bank of 5 different scales at 8 orientations homogeneously distributed in a 7×7 box [13]. 38 local binary patterns (LBP) features were included to quantify homogenous textures [16].

Geometric features describe the segmented sperm cell shapes. We used the Histogram of Gradients [17] with 81 features to quantify the halo shape, including the curvatures and its location relative to the bounding box.

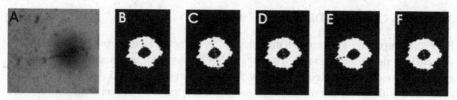

Fig. 2. Morphological feature examples. **A:** Original sperm head image. **B:** Halo diameter. **C:** Total diameter. **D:** Core diameter. **E:** Halo major axis. **F:** Core minor axis.

2.3 Automated Classification

The feature vector of every sperm cell was labeled as fragmented or non-fragmented. A GT dataset was used to train a Support Vector Machine (SVM) classifier for the automatic distinction of two classes: fragmented and non-fragmented. Overall predictive performance was issued using three types of assessments: 100% dataset for training, 10-fold cross-validation, and 70% training/30% testing split. The assessment with 100% training is normally used to observe if the selected features allow splitting the datasets. The 10-fold cross-validation approach randomly split sperm cells data into 10 subsets (9 subsets used for training; 1 subset, for testing). The testing subset was changed until all the subsets were tested (i.e. 10 combinations). Mean classification accuracy was calculated as the average over the subset combination results. In the same way, the dataset was randomly split into 70% training/30% testing subsets, obtaining the accuracy of the performance of classifying the testing subset, which contained instances unknown by the classifier. Since the GT dataset is highly imbalanced, with ~4x the number of non-fragmented over fragmented sperm cells, one imbalanced and one balanced dataset for training and testing were defined for comparison. The classification and testing were implemented with Weka software (Waikato U.; NZ) ver. 3.8.2, using a SMO classifier with polynomial kernel, exponent 1.

3 Experiments

3.1 Subjects

Sperm samples were collected via masturbation from 11 male volunteers (18–56 years old). For each sample a seminal analysis from fresh samples was performed, following the guide for examination [33]. All volunteers consulted for infertility in the Hospital. The samples had a concentration >5 million per ml (severe oligozoosperm) and volume >0.5 ml. Volunteers signed informed consent, approved by Ethics Committee.

3.2 Sperm Chromatin Dispersion Test (SCDt)

For each sample, we performed a modified SCDt using the Halosperm kit [14]. Aliquots of well-liquefied semen were used to assess DNA damage. Approximately 1.5–2 millions sperm cells were suspended in 1% low melting point agarose and deposited on slides pretreated with 0.75% agarose. Next, smears were treated with an acid solution (kit solution 1) to denature DNA for 7 min, a lysis solution (kit solution 2) to remove nuclear proteins for 20 min, and then stained with Wright's stain for 5 min 1:1 with PBS buffer. In response to this treatment, fragmented sperm DNA fragments released between two break points form a very small halo, and most of the stained chromatin forms a compact, intense spot within the sperm core [10, 11]. Non-fragmented sperm chromatin develops a bigger halo of stained chromatin, easily observable by bright field microscopy. Positive controls were treated with DNAse I. SCDt images were captured from the 11 samples and labeled by three highly trained laboratory personnel (experts) to generate the GT dataset. As control, the samples underwent routine analysis by three other experts, in order to produce the fragmentation value of reference ("% Experts" in Table 1), as the average between their results, obtained from visual inspection of replicated samples.

3.3 Image Acquisition

SCDt images were acquired with a bright-field Axio Lab A1 microscope (Carl Zeiss, Jena, Germany) and 20X/N.A. 0.45, Aplan objective lens. We captured 30 images in different fields per sample, containing approximately 400 sperm cells total. A Basler scA780-54gc camera (Basler; Ahrensburg, Germany) was attached to the microscope with a 1x C-Mount adapter. The camera was set to capture RGB color images with automatic exposure and white balance. A custom acquisition software was used.

3.4 Ground Truth (GT) Dataset

The GT dataset is composed of 4895 sperm cells in total, which were classified by three experts from different institutions using a majority vote for solving discrepancies obtained directly from the images. The *imbalanced dataset* (original GT dataset) is constituted of 937 fragmented, 3958 non-fragmented sperm cells (4895 total). The imbalance can induce classification bias leading to a better detection of the larger class (non-fragmented). The issue is more severe in our case due to the big difference (more than 4x). We artificially generated a *balanced dataset* by randomly repeating fragmented and selecting non-fragmented samples, producing 2241 fragmented and 2202 non-fragmented sperm cells (4443 total).

4 Results

Training the classifier with 100% of the imbalanced dataset yielded 96.5% accuracy, with only 88.3% accuracy of fragmented sperm cells and 1.6% false positives. Using the balanced dataset, 94.0% accuracy was obtained, with 93.5% fragmented sperm cells correctly classified and 5.5% false positives. To ensure that there was no overfitting of the dataset, a 10-fold cross-validation test was used. Then, 10 classifier training runs were performed using 9 of the generated subsets for training and one subset for testing for spermatozoa-level analysis. The performance of these 10 runs was averaged to calculate the final accuracy and error. After the 10-fold cross-validation with the imbalanced dataset, 95.5% accuracy was obtained. However, 86.1% were correctly classified as fragmented with only 2.2% false positives. Instead, using a balanced dataset led to 93.3% accuracy, with 93.0% of fragmented sperm correctly classified with 6.4% false positives. After a split of 70% training/30% testing of the imbalanced dataset, we obtained 95.2% accuracy, fragmented sperm cells true positive of 85.4% with 2.3% false positives. On the other hand, with the balanced dataset, the performance was 92.6%, and 93.4% of fragmented sperm cells classified with 8.3% false positives.

4.1 Cross-Validation – New Sample Case

We performed cross-validation of the new sample case test (patient-level analysis), by testing the behavior of the complete system with a new (unknown) patient sample, as it

Table 1. New sample case in cross-validation results. Values were calculated using the output labels of the classifier: Percentage of sperm cell detection and its false positive, Percentage of fragmentation including false positive (%Frag + FP), Percentage of fragmentation (%Frag), classification Accuracy, True Positive (TP), False Positive (FP) and Precision for fragmented class. First row: fragmentation percentages determined by the experts in the routine visual analysis. Second row: calculated percentage by the labeled GT. Third-eighth/ninth-fourteenth rows: classification results with the imbalanced/balanced dataset training.

	Patient	P1	P2	P3	P4	P5	P6	P7	P8	P9	P10	P11	Avg
	% of Detection	84.1	93.7	95.0	95.0	92.5	89.7	90.1	96.2	61.4	93.6	86.3	88.9
	% Detection FP	16.0	15.1	4.4	9.3	9.1	8.7	12.4	8.7	7.6	8.0	5.7	11.5
	% Expert	14.0	9.0	16.0	22.0	26.0	19.0	12.0	10.0	10.0	12.0	11.0	14.6
	% Frag. GT	11.7	5.6	22.1	32.0	30.2	29.2	11.9	11.5	12.1	15.9	15.3	17.9
I m b a l a n c e d	%Frag + FP	16.2	16.9	18.2	27.2	25.1	26.8	9.5	8.1	11.8	11.6	11.8	16.7
	% Frag	14.2	6.8	15.1	28.2	25.2	25.8	9.1	7.3	12.1	10.5	11.6	15.1
	Accuracy (%)	95.8	97.9	95.1	94.2	94.4	91.3	97.9	96.9	94.8	95.3	95.1	95.3
	TP Rate Frag (%)	90.2	92.3	76.4	87.6	85.6	90.6	85.2	71.1	76.9	72.2	74.0	82.0
	FP Rate Frag (%)	3.4	1.8	0.4	3.0	2.3	8.5	0.6	0.2	2.6	1.2	1.5	2.3
	Precision Frag (%)	78.7	75.0	97.7	92.5	93.4	73.8	93.9	97.0	81.1	89.7	88.5	87.4
B a l a n c e d	%Frag + FP	18.5	22.3	19.2	37.9	29.1	38.4	12.1	9.5	15.5	15.3	13.6	21.0
	% Frag	16.0	12.3	19.0	38.9	29.3	37.7	11.6	8.8	15.4	14.4	13.5	19.7
	Accuracy (%)	94.0	91.5	94.7	89.7	94.4	83.3	96.3	97.1	93.4	95.3	94.7	93.0
	TP Rate Frag (%)	90.2	84.6	85.5	98.2	93.2	100	88.9	80.0	84.6	80.6	79.5	87.8
	FP Rate Frag	5.5	8.1	3.1	13.9	5.2	21.1	2.9	1.0	5.3	4.6	2.9	6.7
	Precision Frag (%)	69.8	37.9	87.0	75.0	87.2	55.8	77.4	90.0	70.2	72.5	81.7	73.2

would occur in a clinical setting corresponding to patient-level analysis. The 11 possible combinations were tested, with results shown in Table 1. For the balanced/imbalanced dataset, the minimum accuracy was 83.3%/91.3%, and the average was 93.0%/95.3%. As the fragmentation percentage of the sample is the clinically most relevant value, we calculated the differences of fragmentation percentage relative to GT, in order to predict the clinical behavior. The average difference of fragmentation percentage for the balanced/imbalanced dataset was 3.55%/3.64%, with 8.52%/6.93% worst-case value. The average difference with respect to the GT including the false positive in the detection step was 4.61%/4.17% for balanced/imbalanced training dataset, with a maximum difference of 16.75%/11.35%.These results show that the worst result is greater than 10%, but on average the value is lower than 10%[1].

5   Discussion and Conclusion

An accurate, automated classification of sperm cell halos to quantify DNA fragmentation in SCDt images of human sperm, enables reliable diagnosing and assessing of the severity of DNA damage. Our presented method show an accurate, objective, and non-biased manner fragmentation analysis, independently of the laboratory personnel. We introduced an automated, reproducible method for the segmentation and classification of halos in digital SCDt images that we found to be feasible and accurate for clinical application. Microptic [21] and Hamilton-Throne [15] provide automated detectors, but without published method details or performance evaluations to allow for comparisons. In the literature, there is a few reported results having similar results compared to our proposed algorithm [10, 35, 36].

From the two training strategy datasets, we found that the imbalanced dataset produced the best performing SVM classifier, with results comparable to human experts. No bias was used when selecting the samples and images for evaluation, which supports the classifier's robustness against typical variations in the sample appearance that can be caused by artefacts from the slide preparation or the acquisition process. The classifier works in a manner that is able to learn various types of features of the halo region. With regards to time consumption, SCDt images can be taken in 5 min, and the implemented algorithm took approximately 15 min compared to visual inspection that takes 15–30 min, depending on the technician's expertise. The time reduction was not significant, but in routine work the visual inspection time is enough to acquire three samples for automated classification. Further gains can be attained if the algorithm implementation is focused on computation time instead of prototyping, as is the case of the present implementation. It is worth noting that the maximum difference of the fragmented cells percentage obtained with our method is close to the 10% indicated by the WHO guide for clinical laboratories [33], and lower on average. Our results suggest that the best classifier is obtained with the imbalanced training dataset, due to its better accuracy. We think that it would be feasible to consider the automated assessment of sperm DNA fragmentation by SCDt, in order to obtain objective and comparable results among andrology

---

[1] 10% of maximum error is recommended by the World Health Organization for clinical laboratories in the reported values [34].

and reproductive medicine laboratories. Future work to improve the classification performance can be done to include tail detection, and to train the system only with sperm cells that have tail, in addition to the additional features (see supplemental material).

Supplementary Figures and Tables

(See Figs. 3, 4 and 5, Tables 2 and 3).

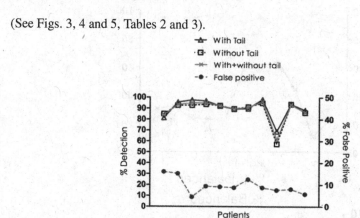

Fig. 3. Percentage of detected sperm with respect to the gold standard for the case of sperm cells with, without, and with+without tail. The percentage of false positive detection corresponds to objects wrongly labeled as spermatozoa (e.g. debris, artefacts, or rounded cells).

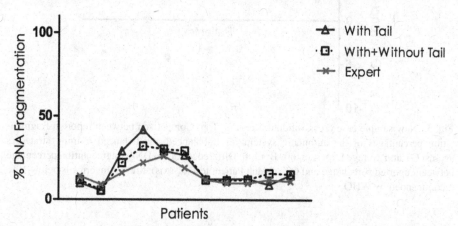

Fig. 4. Percentage of sperm DNA fragmentation in GT including: i) sperm cells with tail, ii) all sperm cells (with and without tail), and iii) expert reference value (visual analysis). The graph shows similar values of calculated % of DNA fragmentation using sperm cells with and with+without tail.

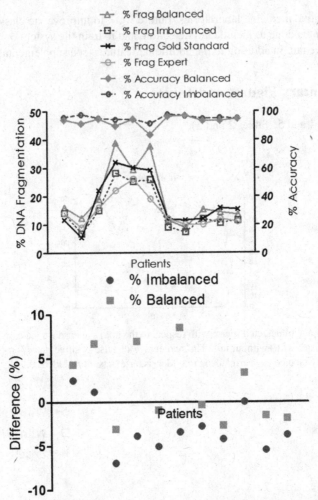

Fig. 5. New sample case cross validation results. Top: Comparison between reported fragmentation percentages of the automatic system for imbalanced and balanced training strategies against GT and average Expert report. Bottom: Differences of the DNA fragmentation percentage between reported percentage and GT of each Patient test (X-axis). Maximum error is below 10% recommended by WHO.

Table 2. Ground Truth (GT) dataset and Detection results. GT dataset was manually counted for 3 experts from acquired images, obtaining final classification of every sperm cell using majority vote. Percentage of fragmented sperm cells for the case of cells with tail (w) and the case including with and without tail (w+wo) are shown. For each one, the number of fragmented, non-fragmented and the total of evaluated sperm cells for 11 patients (P1–11) included in the GT dataset are shown. Percentages of detected sperm cells compared to GT for the cases of cells with (w) and with+without (w+wo) tail are shown. Also, the number of detected objects that do not correspond to a sperm cell (detection false positive percentage) is presented.

		P1		P2		P3		P4		P5		P6	
		w+wo	w	w+wo	w	w+wo	w	w+wo	w	w+wo	w	w+wo	w
GT	% of Frag. sperm	11.7	9.9	5.6	5.5	22.1	29.0	32.0	41.9	30.2	29.1	29.2	26.8
	# Frag. Sperms	46	28	14	10	66	49	128	101	157	114	82	65
	# Not Frag. Sperms	349	254	238	172	233	120	272	140	363	278	199	178
	# Total Sperms	395	282	252	182	299	169	400	241	520	392	281	243
Detection	% of Detection	84.1	85.1	93.7	92.9	95.0	92.9	95.0	93.8	92.5	92.6	89.7	89.7
	% False Positive	16.0		15.11		4,38		9.31		9.1		8.7	
	# False Positive	63		42		13		39		48		24	

		P7		P8		P9		P10		P11		Total	
		w+wo	w	w+wo	w	w+wo	w	w+wo	w	w+wo	w	w+wo	w
GT	% of Frag. sperm	11.9	12.3	11.5	12.4	12.1	12.6	15.9	9.1	15.3	14.9	17.8	18.2
	# Frag. Sperms	70	47	54	37	60	41	47	15	93	76	855	608
	# Not Frag. Sperms	520	336	416	262	437	285	248	150	515	436	3958	2730
	# Total Sperms	590	383	470	299	497	326	295	165	608	512	4813	3338
Detection	% of Detection	90.1	91.4	96.2	95.0	61.4	57.4	93.6	93.9	86.5	86.3	88.9	88.3
	% False Positive	12.4		8.7		7.6		8.0		5.7		9.5	
	# False Positive	76		43		25		24		32		39	

Table 3. Automated sperm cell evaluation results spermatozoa-level analysis. Classification accuracy obtained after SVM classifier training using the complete imbalanced or balanced datasets. First column: results the of the SVM classifier with 100% of the dataset used for training. Second column: results with 10-fold cross validation (random splitting). Third column: results with the dataset randomly split in 70% training/30% testing. The values of Accuracy, True Positive (TP), False Positive (FP), and Precision for Fragmented sperm classification; and difference between GT and classified % of fragmented sperm cells are presented.

	100% Training		Cross Validation 10-fold		70% Training / 30% Testing	
	Imbalanced	Balanced	Imbalanced	Balanced	Imbalanced	Balanced
Accuracy (%)	96.5	94.0	95.5	93.3	95.2	92.6
TP Rate Frag (%)	88.3	93.5	86.1	93.0	85.4	93.4
FP Rate Frag (%)	1.6	5.5	2.2	6.4	2.3	8.3
Precision (%)	92.8	94.5	90.6	93.7	90.1	92.2
Difference (%)	0.92	0.56	0.97	0.36	1.05	0.68

References

1. Agarwal, A., Cho, C.L., Esteves, S.C.: Should we evaluate and treat sperm DNA fragmentation? Curr. Opin. Obstet. Gynecol. **28**(3), 164–171 (2016)
2. Auger, J., et al.: Intra- and inter-individual variability in human sperm concentration, motility and vitality assessment during a workshop involving ten laboratories. Hum. Reprod. **15**(11), 2360–2368 (2000)
3. Bakos, H.W., Thompson, J.G., Feil, D., Lane, M.: Sperm DNA damage is associated with assisted reproductive technology pregnancy. Int. J. Androl. **31**(5), 518–526 (2008)
4. Benchaib, M., Lornage, J., Mazoyer, C., Lejeune, H., Salle, B., François, G.J.: Sperm deoxyribonucleic acid fragmentation as a prognostic indicator of assisted reproductive technology outcome. Fertil. Steril. **87**(1), 93–100 (2007)
5. Bungum, M., Humaidan, P., Spano, M., Jepson, K., Bungum, L., Giwercman, A.: The predictive value of sperm chromatin structure assay (SCSA) parameters for the outcome of intrauterine insemination, IVF and ICSI. Hum. Reprod. **19**(6), 1401–1408 (2004)
6. Carrell, D.T., et al.: Sperm DNA fragmentation is increased in couples with unexplained recurrent pregnancy loss. Arch. Androl. **49**(1), 49–55 (2003)
7. Check, J.H., Graziano, V., Cohen, R., Krotec, J., Check, M.L.: Effect of an abnormal sperm chromatin structural assay (SCSA) on pregnancy outcome following (IVF) with ICSI in previous IVF failures. Arch. Androl. **51**(2), 121–124 (2005)
8. Daris, B., Goropevsek, A., Hojnik, N., Vlaisavljević, V.: Sperm morphological abnormalities as indicators of DNA fragmentation and fertilization in ICSI. Arch. Gynecol. Obstet. **281**(2), 363–367 (2010)
9. Fernández, J.L., et al.: Simple determination of human sperm DNA fragmentation with an improved sperm chromatin dispersion test. Fertil. Steril. **84**(4), 833–842 (2005)
10. Fernández, J.L., et al.: Halosperm® is an easy, available, and cost-effective alternative for Ddetermining sperm DNA fragmentation. Fertil. Steril. **84**(4), 86 (2005)

11. Fernández, J.L., Muriel, L., Rivero, M.T., Goyanes, V., Vazquez, R., Alvarez, J.G.: The sperm chromatin dispersion test: a simple method for the determination of sperm DNA fragmentation. J. Androl. **24**(1), 59–66 (2003)

12. Gosálvez, J., et al.: Characterisation of a subpopulation of sperm with massive nuclear damage, as recognised with the sperm chromatin dispersion test. Andrologia **46**(6), 602–609 (2013)

13. Haghighat, M., Zonouz, S., Abdel-Mottaleb, M.: Identification using encrypted biometrics. In: Wilson, R., Hancock, E., Bors, A., Smith, W. (eds.) CAIP 2013. LNCS, vol. 8048, pp. 440–448. Springer, Heidelberg (2013). https://doi.org/10.1007/978-3-642-40246-3_55

14. Halotech DNA: Halosperm® (2016). http://www.halotechdna.com/productos/halosperm/

15. Hamilton-Throne Inc.: DNA fragmentation software (2016). http://www.hamiltonthorne. com/index.php/dna-fragmentation-software-2

16. Heikkila, M., Pietikainen, M.: A texture-based method for modeling the background and detecting moving objects. IEEE Trans. Pattern. Anal. Mach. Intell. **28**(4), 657–662 (2006)

17. Ludwig O., Delgado D., Goncalves V., Nunes U.: Trainable classifier-fusion schemes: an application to pedestrian detection. In: ITSC, pp. 1–6 (2009)

18. Larson, K.L., DeJonge, C.J., Barnes, A.M., Jost, L.K., Evenson, D.P.: Sperm chromatin structure assay parameters as predictors of failed pregnancy following assisted reproductive techniques. Hum. Reprod. **15**(8), 1717–1722 (2000)

19. Leushuis, E., et al.: Reproducibility and reliability of repeated semen analyses in male partners of subfertile couples. Fertil. Steril. **94**(7), 2631–2635 (2010)

20. Li, Z., Wang, L., Cai, J., Huang, H.: Correlation of sperm DNA damage with IVF and ICSI outcomes: a systematic review and meta-analysis. J. Assist. Reprod. Genet. **23**(9–10), 367–376 (2006)

21. Microptic S.L.: Automatic diagnostic system, SCA DNA fragmentation (2016). http://www. micropticsl.com/products/sperm-class-analyzer-casa-system/analysis-modules/sca-dna-fra gmentation/

22. Nasr-Esfahani, M.H., Razavi, S., Vahdati, A.A., Fathi, F., Tavalaee, M.: Evaluation of sperm selection procedure based on hyaluronic acid binding ability on ICSI outcome. J. Assist. Reprod. Genet. **25**(5), 197–203 (2008)

23. Oleszczuk, K., Giwercman, A., Bungum, M.: Sperm chromatin structure assay in prediction of *in vitro* fertilization outcome. Andrology. **4**(2), 290–296 (2016)

24. Parinaud, J., Mieusset, R., Vieitez, G., Labal, B., Richoilley, G.: Influence of sperm parameters on embryo quality. Fertil. Steril. **60**(5), 888–892 (1993)

25. Sakkas, D., Alvarez, J.G.: Sperm DNA fragmentation: mechanisms of origin, impact on reproductive outcome, and analysis. Fertil. Steril. **93**(4), 1027–1036 (2010)

26. Saleh, R.A., et al.: Negative effects of increased sperm DNA damage in relation to seminal oxidative stress in men with idiopathic and male factor infertility. Fertil. Steril. **79**(3), 1597–1605 (2003)

27. Saxena, P., et al.: Possible role of male factors in recurrent pregnancy loss. Indian J. Physiol. Pharmacol. **52**(3), 274–282 (2008)

28. Seli, E., Gardner, D.K., Schoolcraft, W.B., Moffatt, O., Sakkas, D.: Extent of nuclear DNA damage in ejaculated spermatozoa impacts on blastocyst development after *in vitro* fertilization. Fertil. Steril. **82**(2), 378–383 (2004)

29. Simon, L., Brunborg, G., Stevenson, M., Lutton, D., McManus, J., Lewis, S.E.: Clinical significance of sperm DNA damage in assisted reproduction outcome. Hum. Reprod. **25**(7), 1594–1608 (2010)

30. Spanò M., Bonde J.P., Hjøllund H.I., Kolstad H.A., Cordelli E., Leter G.: Sperm chromatin damage impairs human fertility. The Danish first pregnancy planner study team. Fertil. Steril. **73**(1), 43–50 (2000)

31. Trisini, A.T., Singh, S.M., Duty, S.M., Hauser, R.: Relationship between human semen parameters and deoxyribonucleic acid damage assessed by the neutral comet assay. Fertil. Steril. **82**(6), 1623–1632 (2004)

32. de la Calle, J.F.V., et al.: Sperm deoxyribonucleic acid fragmentation as assessed by the sperm chromatin dispersion test in assisted reproductive technology programs: results of a large prospective multicenter study. Fertil. Steril. **90**(5), 1792–1799 (2008)

33. World Health Organization: Laboratory manual for the examination and processing of human semen, 5th edn. (2010). http://whqlibdoc.who.int/publications/2010/9789241547789_eng.pdf

34. Zini, A., Boman, J.M., Belzile, E., Ciampi, A.: Sperm DNA damage is associated with an increased risk of pregnancy loss after IVF and ICSI: systematic review and meta-analysis. Hum. Reprod. **23**(12), 2663–2668 (2008)

35. Banu Rekha, B., Vidyalakshmi, S., Sree Niranjanaa Bose, S., Anusha Devi, T.T.: Image processing methods for automated assessment of sperm DNA integrity. In: Verma, N.K., Ghosh, A.K. (eds.) Computational Intelligence: Theories, Applications and Future Directions—Volume I. AISC, vol. 798, pp. 109–117. Springer, Singapore (2019). https://doi.org/10.1007/978-981-13-1132-1_9

36. Dimitriadis, I., et al.: Automated smartphone-based system for measuring sperm viability, DNA fragmentation, and hyaluronic binding assay score. PLoS ONE **14**(3), e0212562 (2019). https://doi.org/10.1371/journal.pone.0212562

Machine Vision-Based Expert System for Automated Skin Cancer Detection

Masum Shah Junayed[1,2](✉) [ID], Afsana Ahsan Jeny[1] [ID], Lavdie Rada[1] [ID],
and Md Baharul Islam[1,3] [ID]

[1] Department of Computer Engineering, Bahcesehir University, Istanbul, Turkey
masumshahjunayed@gmail.com
[2] Department of CSE, Daffodil International University, Dhaka, Bangladesh
[3] College of Data Science and Engineering, American University of Malta, Cospicua, Malta

Abstract. Skin cancer is the most frequently occurring kind of cancer, accounting for about one-third of all cases. Automatic early detection without expert intervention for a visual inspection would be of great help for society. The image processing and machine learning methods have significantly contributed to medical and biomedical research, resulting in fast and exact inspection in different problems. One of such problems is accurate cancer detection and classification. In this study, we introduce an expert system based on image processing and machine learning for skin cancer detection and classification. The proposed approach consists of three significant steps: pre-processing, feature extraction, and classification. The pre-processing step uses the grayscale conversion, Gaussian filter, segmentation, and morphological operation to represent skin lesion images better. We employ two feature extractors, i.e., the ABCD scoring method (asymmetry, border, color, diameter) and gray level co-occurrence matrix (GLCM), to extract cancer-affected areas. Finally, five different machine learning classifiers such as logistic regression (LR), decision tree (DT), k-nearest neighbors (KNN), support vector machine (SVM), and random forest (RF) used to detect and classify skin cancer. Experimental results show that random forest exceeds all other classifiers achieving an accuracy of 97.62% and 0.97 Area Under Curve (AUC), which is state-of-the-art on the experimented open-source dataset PH2.

Keywords: Skin cancer · ABCD rules · GLCM · Morphological operations · Image processing · Machine learning

1 Introduction

Cancer, an uncontrollable cell division in a body region, is one of the greatest challenges in contemporary medicine. The nutrients absorbed by cancer cells alongside the healthy cells make them get more potent and as a result, the body cells became weaker, whereas the immune system can not help defending those body cells. The metastasis of these cancer cells may go from one area of the body to other places. The liver, lungs, bones, breasts, prostates, bladders, and rectums may all be affected by cancer, as the skin [1].

Skin cancer classifies as melanoma and non-melanoma. Melanoma is the fastest-growing type of skin cancer and causes the majority of fatalities. As reported by WHO,

© Springer Nature Switzerland AG 2022
C. Brito-Loeza et al. (Eds.): ISICS 2022, CCIS 1569, pp. 83–96, 2022.
https://doi.org/10.1007/978-3-030-98457-1_7

non-melanoma skin cancers were found in two to three million people, while melanoma skin cancers occurred in 132,000 people annually worldwide [2]. After the skin cancer identification, one can treat it with radiation treatment, chemotherapy, immunotherapy, or a combination of these methods. For better treatment results early identification is crucial. The early detection of skin cancer is possible as the skin changes are easily visible. On the other hand, having an automated system that helps to diagnose the type of cancer during the early phase without the require of a trained specialist would be of great help. Without blood sample requirements or a trained specialist, computer-aid solutions are required.

In the past decade, considerable study on the automated categorization of skin lesions and skin cancer diagnosis using machine learning, particularly feature extraction based methods, has been explored. Some significant works, commonly employed by professionals, are ABCD rule evaluation [3] or the 7-point checklist [4], which serves as the starting input for either a deterministic or model-based categorization system. Many studies have been published to assist in early melanoma identification. The bulk of this research concluded that benign lesions and malignant tumors could not be effectively differentiated because of missing characteristics. To solve such an issue, researchers have been looking into specific identification of characteristics or features. Recent papers such as [1,5–7] proposed systems to classify skin cancers. For example, in [6], the authors used GLCM for feature extraction and SVM and RF for classification, But their accuracy was low, only 89.31% due to the absence of the image pre-processing steps. As a result, the misclassification rates were increased. Banasode et al. [1] proposed another system to detect melanoma skin cancer through only SVM and some pre-processing steps and got an accuracy of 96.9%. Ozkan et al. [8] proposed a skin lesion categorization method. They use four machine learning techniques to identify the lesion as melanoma, abnormal, or normal, with ANN achieving the best accuracy rate of 92.50%. Waheed et al. [9] suggested classifying melanoma by proposing a machine learners model based on the discrimination of characteristics such as various skin lesion color and structure features. Their accuracy of 96% compiled the previous models. Although the accuracy of the above-mentioned works is good still skin cancer images are misclassified in the absence of the proper proposed system. Besides, it is necessary to enhance the performance of skin cancer detection and classification methods. The main contributions of this work follow as:

- We introduce a new expert system for the automated detection of skin cancer in which the pre-processing, feature extraction, and classifiers are employed.
- The grayscale conversion, Gaussian filter, Otsu's and global thresholding segmentation methods and morphological operations are applied in pre-processing stages to better represent skin cancer images and segment the particular region of skin cancer.
- In order to perform the classification process efficiently, we implemented a feature fusion procedure in our system, in which the ABCD rules and GLCM techniques are extracted simultaneously to get correct feature information after segmenting the particular region of skin cancer images.
- Five different machine learning classifiers have been utilized for skin cancer detection. Compared results between the explored classifiers and to the prior approaches

have been shown. This work concludes in the achievement of state-of-the-art results with an accuracy of 97.62% by Random Forest.

The rest of the paper is discussed as follows: Sect. 2 includes related works, Sect. 3 gives details on materials and methods, Sect. 4 shows the experimental results, in Sect. 5 we discuss on the results, and Sect. 6 concludes the paper.

2 Related Works

Recently, numerous automated computer-aided techniques have been purposed in the field of medical image analysis. They have been widely used as disease detection, recognition, and classification systems through which the remote screening of the diseases have been possible with high diagnosis accuracy. These systems are generally divided into two main groups, i.e. machine learning-based and deep learning-based approaches, that been applied on various tasks of eye-disease [10], MRI image analysis [11], cancer recognition [1], skin disease [12], etc. In This section, we focus on the recent works published for skin cancer based on machine learning and image processing techniques. N. Garg et al. [13] proposed employing image processing techniques to identify melanoma skin cancer. They used the ABCD rule, which stands for Asymmetry, Border Irregularity, Color, and Diameter. Matlab's imfilter, imadjust, and median filter functions are used to apply illumination adjustment during the preprocessing step. After the preprocessing procedure, the skin lesion segmentation was completed. Finally, the features were extracted using the ABCD rule. They were able to improve the accuracy to 91.6%. Pham et al. [14] used Deep CNN with Data Augmentation to classify skin lesions. To prepare the dataset, they combined photos from several sources such as the ISBI Challenge, the ISIC Archive, and the PH2 dataset. The model architecture was InceptionV4, and the results were compared using Support Vector Machine (SVM), Random Forest (RF), and Neural Network (NN) classifiers. They were able to obtain an overall accuracy rate of 89%. Despite the fact that the model architecture was InceptionV4, the accuracy attained was insufficient. Jordan et al. [15] suggested a deep learning-based technique for classifying multimodal skin lesions. They used 2917 cases from five categories to create their dataset. As a model architecture, they employed a modified ResNet-50. They modified the algorithm by removing the softmax and fully connected layers at the end and replacing the flattened output with a 2048-dimensional image feature vector, which they called image feature extraction network in their article. Following the evaluation, single image classification accuracy was determined to be 85.8% on average, with multimodal network accuracy being 86.6%. The multimodal network methodology does not achieve a high level of precision. Serban et al. [16] used a CNN to help in automatic skin cancer diagnosis. A total of 1000 photos were gathered from the International Skin Imaging Collaboration and the PH2 databases. There are 500 photos in each of the two classes: benign tumors and cutaneous malignant lesions. The dataset was subjected to a skin segmentation algorithm. The dataset was then input into a neural network. On the dataset, the recommended solution had an accuracy of 80.52%. The dataset was small, and the precision was even lower. Mengistu et al. [17] have devised an algorithm that combines the Self-Organizing Map (SOM) with the Radial Basis Function (RBF) to pinpoint the exact site of skin cancer. Their main goal was to use the minimum required image analysis to distinguish between different types of skin cancer Hairs, bubbles, and other similar items will frequently appear in dermoscopic vision. They improved the quality of the cancer photos before using MATLAB to recognize the image. The overall classification accuracy was 93.15% after feature extraction. Barata et al. [18] used the Gaussian mixtures approach in this work to detect colors in lesions dermoscopy images, which is a suggested technique for detection and recognition in cancers dermoscopy images. When physicians diagnose dermoscopy pictures by applying the ABCD rule, they assert that hues such as black, blue, gray, white, and red are more frequent in melanomas than in benign lesions. The detection of a blue-whitish veil is used in Computer-Assisted Diagnosis (CAD) systems to determine whether a lesion is cancerous or benign. When the information from the HSV and $L * a * b$ color spaces is combined, the outcome is 78.8%, according to the researchers.

3   Materials and Methods

In this section, we described our workflow and details of our work. The whole process combines several steps which are described in the following. Figure 1 illustrates the overall workflow of our model.

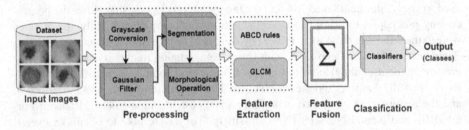

Fig. 1. The architecture of our proposed system. We used resized images as the input in this case. Then, we applied grayscale conversion, a Gaussian filter, Otsu's segmentation approach, and morphological procedures (erosion and dilation) in the pre-processing stage. For feature extraction, ABCD rules and GLCM are utilized, simultaneously. Then, extracted features are fused as a feature fusion. Finally, five different machine learning based classifiers such as Logistic Regression, Decision Tree, KNN, SVM, and Random Forest were then used to classify, detect and evaluate skin cancer.

3.1   Dataset

The evaluation of the proposed model is done through the public accessible dataset PH2 [19]. It includes 200 images separated into three categories: 80 benign lesions, 80 atypical lesions, and 40 melanoma lesions. The database of all images has RGB color with 768×560 pixels. The Universidade do Porto in Ecnico Lisboa (also known as the Porto School of Engineering) partnered with the Dermatology Service of Hospital Pedro Hispano in Matosinhos, Portugal, to build the PH2 database. We utilize 200 images for our study, randomly picked, to generalize our approach. The database includes 40 melanomas and 160 benign images.

3.2 Dataset Pre-processing

This step incorporates both image preparation and image enhancement techniques. Picture preprocessing is a time-consuming method due to the large number of filters that must be applied in sequence to the whole original picture to separate the valuable information from the noise and boost specific crucial image properties for the implementation. Grayscale conversion, noise reduction, picture enhancement, and thresholding are the four major components of this step. Each sort of noise must be eliminated in the noise reduction step before going on to the feature extraction step, as is evident from the preceding paragraph. More specifically, due to the lighting circumstances associated with visual media, two typical forms of noise are identified: hairs and dark-colored segments.

Image Resize. As a first step we downsized the photos to a dimension of 52×52 pixels in order to speed up processing while keeping the critical portions intact.

Grayscale Conversion. To transform colored to gray-scale images without destroying important information a weighted sum approach can be used. The following is a representation of its most regularly used Eq. (1):

$$Grayscale - intensity = 0.299R + 0.587G + 0.114B \qquad (1)$$

The transformation of the original image to grayscale can help the image processing step operate better. Colored images are more complicated and time-consuming to modify.

Gaussian Filter for Noise Removal. Natural variables like hair and tiny particles, as well as external factors such as lighting, reflections, and various recording techniques, are common examples of noise sources [20]. The application of a Gaussian filter is utilized to remove extraneous pixels from images. In this process, unwanted pixels are transformed by determining the average number of the adjoining or covering pixels of unwanted pixels, which is done based on the Gaussian distribution of the pixels in question. The Gaussian filter is a linear filter that is utilized in image processing to decrease the noise level in the images. The 2D Gaussian smoothing operator is shown in Eq. 2:

$$G(x, y) = \frac{1}{2\pi\sigma^2} e^{-\frac{x^2+y^2}{2\sigma^2}} \qquad (2)$$

where σ is the standard deviation.

Segmentation Process. By transforming the image to binary and depicting the area of interest, the image segmentation stage separates the backdrop from the lesion. As the ABCD rule uses binary images to retrieve the images' characteristics, this step seems to be the most important for our approach. When performing medical image analysis, segmentation of images into specific points of research is essential. It is possible to receive accurate results from the interest pixels if the segmentation process is performed correctly. Image segmentation can be accomplished using a variety of methods and algorithms. There are numerous thresholding algorithms to choose from. Among these, the Otsu [21] and global thresholding approaches [22] have been singled out for special mention. Between these two approaches, the most significant distinction is that Otsu's algorithm does automatic image thresholding. Rather than using a global method, which requires a specified thresholding value, it searches for the most efficient thresholding value that minimizes intra-class variation, as is done with the global algorithm. Finding the global thresholding value in a grayscale image may be a simple process if the backdrop and the area of interest have distinct brightness levels in the grayscale image. The global thresholding method is rather simple to put into practice. If the number of pixels is larger than or equal to the global thresholding value, then the pixel will be changed with white pixels, and if the value is below the global thresholding value, the pixel will be substituted with black pixels. The output of the thresholding technique is a white background with a black region corresponding to the lesion. For the morphological operator to be applied we invert the obtained image.

Morphological Operations. The opening operator was found as the most appropriate for this work. This operator is a mixture of two other operators such as erosion and dilation, used successively. This procedure erases tiny white objects while keeping the information about the area of interest. To create the opening operator we need a kernel whose size is dependent on the size of the undesired object being filtered out. We employ a 3×3 kernel for both filters. As a result of this filter, the lesion may be reconstructed to its original size, helping to compute the characteristics from the ABCD rule.

3.3 Feature Extraction

The method of obtaining significant characteristics from skin cancer images is known as feature extraction. Skin cancer images are analyzed using any systems to extract several components that may be used to distinguish between benign and malignant lesions. In the following, we describe the ABCD scoring method [3] feature and GLCM method [11] feature.

Asymmetry (A). Melanomas grow asymmetrically, whereas benign tumors develop symmetrically, according to the medical record. To calculate the asymmetry index we first compute the comparison difference between the lesion picture and its horizontal flip [23]. The same procedure follows between the lesion picture and its vertical flip. Following that, we compute the ratio between each difference and the entire lesion area and preserve the average values of those ratios. Equation (3) illustrates asymmetry:

$$Asymmetry = \frac{\frac{Image_{area}-hflip_{area}}{Image_{area}} + \frac{Image_{area}-vflip_{area}}{Image_{area}}}{2} \tag{3}$$

Border Irregularity (B). The boundaries of the lesion are depicted by the edge pixels resulting from the lesion segmentation [24]. The lesion area is split into eight equal sections, and the regions of the lesion that have a sharp cut are computed. The border's degree is between 0 and 8. The value of zero is obtained from the regular component, whereas the value of one is obtained from the irregular component. Thus, the degree of melanoma ranges from 3 to 8. Product descriptors of vectors and inflection points are employed to extract peaks, valleys, and sharp edges at the borders of a lesion. Small irregular boundaries are evaluated using the inflection spot descriptor. Uneven boundaries are measured using the vector product descriptor, while uncertain uneven boundaries are measured with the scalar products classifier. Equation 4 is used to compute the vector product.

$$V_i = (x_2 - x_1)(y_3 - y_1)(y_2 - y_1)(x_3 - x_1) \qquad (4)$$

where (x_1, y_1), (x_2, y_2) and (x_3, y_3) depict whether the section remains to tops, rectangular shapes or slopes. If $v_i > 0$, it's a top; when $v_i < 0$, it's a plain, when $v_i = 0$ is a solid line.

Color (C). The lesion is reported to come in a variety of hues, including blue, white, black, light, red, brown, and blue-grey, as well as color gradients between dark and light inside the confines of the skin lesion. The variations in dye within a skin lesion boundary are critical for the categorization and segmentation phases of the process. When a lesion picture contains color characteristics, we may assume it is diagnosing melanoma or not.

Diameter (D). Skin cancer cells grow multiple faster than other cells, and the exponential function is used to characterize cancer development. The diameter of the lesion is one of the essential criteria to consider when determining if it is a melanoma or a benign lesion. One of the characteristics used to detect and diagnose a skin lesion is its diameter. Melanoma lesions often have a diameter of more than six millimeters in ABCD rules. It is considered malignant if the diameter is higher than 6 mm in diameter. If the diameter of the lesion is smaller than 6 mm, it is considered innocuous. Equation (5) is used to calculate the diameter of the lesion.

$$D = \sqrt{\frac{4LA}{\pi}} \qquad (5)$$

GLCM is often used for textural analysis, which involves obtaining the dispersed intensity of an item. GLCM examines two pixels, one of which is a neighbour and the other of which is a reference. Contrast, correlation, energy, entropy, homogeneity, prominence, and shade are all produced using GLCM. In this experiment, we used the most effective characteristics in GLCM, which are Contrast (C), Correlation (ρ), Energy (E), Homogeneity (H), and Entropy (K) [11].

3.4 Feature Fusion and Classification

The ABCD and GLCM extracted features are combined and fed into machine learning classifiers. After dimensionality reduction, the feature fusion learns characteristics to represent their rich internal information and a compressed description of integrated features. For classification, we used five different machine learning classifiers, including logistic regression (LR), decision tree (DT), KNN, support vector machine (SVM), and random forest (RF), for recognition and classification of skin cancer. We also calculate the Total Dermoscopy Score (TDS) which determines the TDS score, asymmetry, border, color, and diameter, the four critical criteria used in this methodology to extract the final result: the outcome is determined by combining these four factors. Because feature

extraction is the most crucial aspect of categorizing the lesion into benign and malignant, several variants are connected to the criteria of this approach that may be used
to meet project requirements. This section delves into the characteristics of melanoma
detection. After giving any one of the four aspects a value, (A, B, C, and D), the TDS
is computed using the following Eq. 6:

$$TDS = [(A * 1.3) + (B * 0.1) + (C * 0.5) + (D * 0.5)] \tag{6}$$

If TDS < 5.65 then lesion is called Benign.
If TDS ≥ 5.65 then the lesion is called Melanoma.

4 Experiments

4.1 Experimental Setup

An Intel Core i9 CPU operating at 3.60 GHz, 64 GB of RAM, and an NVIDIA Geforce
RTX 2080 Super GPU with 8 GB of video memory were utilized in this experiment. The
skin cancer detection system is identified and evaluated using the python-conda environment on a Windows 10 operating system. Scipy, Matplotlib, Oritogrey, and OpenCV
libraries are used in all experiments executed in the visual studio code editor. We used
5-fold cross-validation to ensure that each sample appeared in the training and test sets
at least once. The performance matrices are used to calculate the average outcomes.

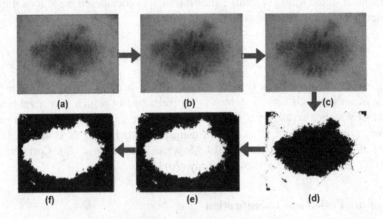

Fig. 2. Step-by-step graphical depiction of data pre-processing. Here (a), (b), (c), (d), (e), and (f)
indicate the resized RGB image, grayscale image, Gaussian filter, Otsu's technique, morphological erosion filter, and morphological dilation filter, respectively.

4.2 Evaluation Details

Here, Fig. 2 represents the stepwise performance of the data preprocessing. At first,
the skin cancer images are resized into 52 × 52 pixels (Fig. 2-a) since we got different resolution images in the PH2 database. Following the resizing of the image, it is

essential to transform the RGB image to a grayscale image, as illustrated in Fig. 2-b. This conversion is achieved using Eq. (1), detailed in-depth in the data preprocessing section's grayscale conversion section. The Gaussian Filter with a 3×3 kernel size is chosen to limit the amount of noise. This decision is based on the Gaussian filter's efforts to avoid edges in the image. When looking at Fig. 2-c, it is clear that the number of hairs has decreased. The following stage is to segment the image, utilizing thresholding procedures. Otsu's strategy is first and foremost chosen, however after specific examinations are reasoned that the global thresholding technique accomplishes similar outcomes since the choice of thresholding esteem is a simple process because of how the pixel values of the lesion are distinguishable from the backdrop. To be more specific, the thresholding esteem is 100. As a result, Otsu's method of determining the propel thresholding value is rendered superfluous. Figure 2-d depicts a binary representation of the image. Notice that the background is white, and the lesion region is black, as can be seen in the image. Particular OpenCV functions, such as those used to extract some feature values, require a black backdrop and a white lesion region to perform effectively. It can be seen in the inverted image that there is still some noise present, indicating that a further image processing step is required. The open morphological filter is introduced into the process to improve the thresholding stage and reduce noise. The kernel size for the open filter has been determined to be 3×3. The open filter uses an erode filter to reduce the size of the white elements in the lesion. The dilation filter is used to restore the lesion to its original size after it has been reconstructed. Figure 2-(e, f) shows that the noise from the preceding photo has been almost eliminated using erosion and dilation, respectively.

4.3 Evaluation Matrix

The Evaluation Matrix summarizes the effectiveness of the algorithm with real-world data. To observe the quality of the model, we provided our model in a Confusion Matrix format. The Confusion Matrix's function is to assess specific characteristics of the model in order to gain a better understanding of its actual performance. True Positive (TP), True Negative (TN), False Positive (FP), and False Negative (FN) values were used to compute: Precision ($\frac{(TP)}{(TP+FP)}$), Accuracy ($\frac{(TP+TN)}{(TP+TN+FP+FN)}$), Specificity ($\frac{(TN)}{(FP+TN)}$), Sensitivity ($\frac{(TP)}{(TP+FN)}$), false-positive rate (FPR= $\frac{(FP)}{(FP+TN)}$), and false-negative rate (FNR= $\frac{(FN)}{(TP+FN)}$).

5 Results and Discussions

5.1 Performance of the Proposed System

Table 1 represents the performance analysis of the feature extraction methods: ABCD and GLCM in testing. From this table, it can be observed that five ML algorithms worked very well on we utilized the ABCD and GLCM methods together. For example, RF achieved 97.62% accuracy while only in ABCD and GLCM it was 94.63% and 95.04% respectively. Similarly, when ABCD and GLCM are used together in LR,

Table 1. The performance of the feature selection methods in the proposed system.

Features	Classifier's					
	RF (%)	SVM (%)	KNN (%)	DT (%)	LR (%)	TDS
ABCD	94.63	90.21	91.01	93.89	89.00	90.03%
GLCM	95.04	92.67	90.87	91.32	91.67	–
ABCD + GLCM	**97.62**	**96.35**	**94.63**	**94.58**	**93.02**	–

4.02% more accuracy was obtained from only ABCD (93.02% vs. 89.00%) and 1.35% more accuracy from only GLCM (93.02% vs. 91.67%) in this experiment.

Figure 3 represents the performance of the accuracy vs. loss graph of RF. The left one represents the loss graph, and the right one is the accuracy graph, respectively. In this experiment, we have used 120 epochs. From this graph, we can say that the loss of RF is decreasing gradually while the accuracy is increasing up to 97.62%. That means our system works well through RF without facing any overfitting issues because of a novel feature fusion approach and a pre-processing phase in our expert system.

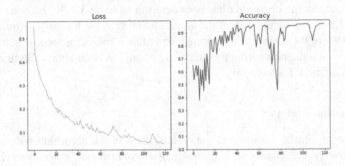

Fig. 3. Accuracy vs. loss graph of the proposed method through random forest classifier.

Table 2. The performance of several machine learning classifiers and TDS value are compared. This table displays ML classifiers' accuracy, precision, sensitivity, specificity, FPR, and FNR.

Classifiers	Accuracy (%)	Precision (%)	Sensitivity (%)	Specificity (%)	FPR (%)	FNR (%)
TDS	90.00	72.50	76.32	93.21	6.79	23.68
LR	93.02	96.25	95.06	84.21	15.79	4.94
DT	94.58	96.35	96.89	85.71	14.29	3.11
KNN	94.63	96.32	96.91	86.05	13.95	3.09
SVM	96.35	97.08	**98.22**	90.00	10.00	1.78
RF	**97.62**	**98.79**	98.19	**95.45**	**4.55**	**1.81**

We have found the TDS score, and this score is evaluated through the evaluation matrix. For the TDS, the accuracy, precision, sensitivity, specificity, FPR, and FNR are

90.00%, 72.50%, 76.32%, 93.21%, 6.79%, and 23.68%, respectively which we have shown in Table 2. To make our system more strong, we also applied five machine learning classifiers which are logistic regression, decision tree, KNN, SVM, and random forest. Here, Table 2 represents the performance analysis of five machine learning classifiers: logistic regression, decision tree, KNN, SVM, random forest, and TDS in terms of accuracy, precision, sensitivity, specificity, FPR, and FNR, respectively. From the table, it can be seen that the random forest achieves the best results regarding accuracy (97.62%), precision (98.79%), sensitivity (98.19%), specificity (95.45%), FPR (4.55%), and FNR (1.81%) respectively, all of which are statistically significant. On the other hand, the logistic regression is achieved the lowest outcomes in terms of accuracy (93.02%), precision (96.25%), sensitivity (95.06%), specificity (84.21%), FPR (15.79%), and FNR (4.94%) respectively. Furthermore, the KNN is in the middle position, and it has 2.99% less accurate than the random forest (97.62 vs. 94.63) and 1.61% greater accuracy than logistic regression (94.63 vs. 93.02).

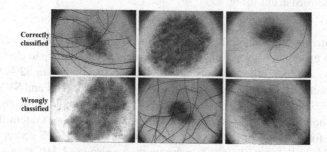

Fig. 4. Examples of some classification results. Here, the first row represents the correctly classified results and second row represents the wrongly classified results of the proposed system.

Some classified and misclassified results are also demonstrated in Fig. 4. From the figure, we can say that sometimes our system can classify the images which consist of thick hairs and sometimes not.

Figure 5 represents the AUC-ROC curve of our proposed system. Here, X and Y-axis represent the false positive rate and true positive rate, respectively. From the ROC curve, it can be said that we got an outstanding result through five ML classifiers in our system. For example, in terms of RF, we got the highest AUC which is 0.97. It indicates that our proposed system has a 97% probability of differentiating the positive and negative classes. On the other hand, in LR, we obtained the lowest AUC, which is 0.90. Whatever our proposed system is showed a competitive performance during this experiment.

5.2 Comparison

Utilizing the PH2 dataset, Table 3 demonstrates a fair comparison in skin cancer detection and classification using machine learning classifiers and image processing methods. The results of specific studies, such as [25–27], that utilized image processing methods

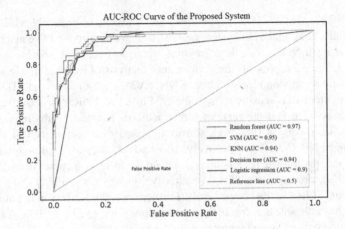

Fig. 5. AUC-ROC curve of the proposed system. Here, the results of the five machine learning classifiers are showed in this figure.

had worse outcomes than those that used machine learning classifiers, as can be seen in this table. For example, Bi et al. [27] used the joint reverse technique to classify the skin cancer classes and found the accuracy, sensitivity, and specificity are 92%, 87.5%, and 93.13%, respectively. On the other hand, [8] and [9] used the ANN and SVM, and they achieved 92.5% and 96% accuracy, respectively. However, another image processing work of Lattoofi et al. [28], who developed an image processing system that utilized ABCD rules for feature extraction and categorized images by TDS score, was recognized for its high accuracy (93.20%). In our work, we also used ABCD rules as feature extraction and TDS score with five machine learning techniques (logistic regression, decision tree, KNN, SVM, and random forest) for classification. Among them, random forest performed outstandingly with an accuracy of 97.62%, precision of 98.79%, sensitivity of 98.19%, and specificity of 95.45%, respectively.

Table 3. Results of the suggested system compared to prior work.

Work done	Years	Classifiers	Precision (%)	Sensitivity (%)	Specificity (%)	Accuracy (%)
G. Arroyo [25]	2015	softmax	–	83.00	95	–
R. Chakravorty [26]	2016	Symmetry type	69.00	67.00	89.00	83.00
L. Bi [27]	2016	Joint Reverse	–	87.50	93.13	92.00
I. A. Ozkan [8]	2017	ANN	92.38	90.86	96.11	92.50
Z. Waheed [9]	2017	SVM	–	97.00	84	96.00
N. F. Lattoofi [28]	2019	TDS	–	90.15	92.59	93.20
Proposed system	2021	**Random Forest**	**98.79**	**98.19**	**95.45**	**97.62**

6   Conclusions and Future Works

In this work, we proposed a system to detect skin cancer: Melanoma and Benign. Two stages are included in the suggested method: the initial pre-processing stage improves the image quality, and accurate detection needs to proceed. First, the grayscale conversion and Gaussian filter improve the images and remove any unwanted pixels from them. Then the otsu's and global threshold methods are applied for segmentation to recognize the region of interest (ROI) in dermoscopy images. Moreover, it is believed that the morphology approach will improve the overall quality of the skin lesion's ROI. To improve the lesion quality, we applied erosion and dilation after the segmentation process. Then, the ABCD rule and GLCM feature extractor are applied to extract affected areas. Finally, we applied the five machine learning classifiers (logistic regression, decision tree, KNN, SVM, and random forest) to detect and classify skin cancer. Experimental results are showed that the random forest outperforms others in terms of accuracy of 97.62% and Area under Curve 0.97, which is promising and state-of-the-art. The time-consuming feature extraction and some misclassifications are the drawbacks of this research. Our future work consists of replacing the time-consuming preprocessing methods with a Convolution Neural Network (CNN) archiştecture. capable to solve the feature extraction issue and expand the dataset's collection with more images.

References

1. Banasode, P., Patil, M., Ammanagi, N.: A melanoma skin cancer detection using machine learning technique: support vector machine. In: IOP Conference Series: Materials Science and Engineering, vol. 1065, pp. 012039. IOP Publishing (2021)
2. Esteva, A., et al.: Dermatologist-level classification of skin cancer with deep neural networks. Nature 542(7639), 115–118 (2017)
3. Messadi, M., Cherifi, H., Bessaid, A.: Segmentation and ABCD rule extraction for skin tumors classification. arXiv preprint arXiv:2106.04372 (2021)
4. Argenziano, G., et al.: Seven-point checklist of dermoscopy revisited. Br. J. Dermatol. 164(4), 785–790 (2011)
5. Jeny, A.A., et al.: SkNet: a convolutional neural networks based classification approach for skin cancer classes. In: 2020 23rd International Conference on Computer and Information Technology (ICCIT), pp. 1–6. IEEE (2020)
6. Murugan, A., Nair, S.A.H., Preethi, A.A.P., Kumar, K.P.S.: Diagnosis of skin cancer using machine learning techniques. Microprocess. Microsyst. 81, 103727 (2021)
7. Junayed, M.S., Anjum, N., Noman, A., Islam, B.: A deep CNN model for skin cancer detection and classification (2021)
8. Ozkan, I.A., Koklu, M.: Skin lesion classification using machine learning algorithms. Int. J. Intell. Syst. Appl. Eng. 5(4), 285–289 (2017)
9. Waheed, Z., Waheed, A., Zafar, M., Riaz, F.: An efficient machine learning approach for the detection of melanoma using dermoscopic images. In: 2017 International Conference on Communication, Computing and Digital Systems (C-CODE), pp. 316–319. IEEE (2017)
10. Junayed, M.S., Islam, M.B., Sadeghzadeh, A., Rahman, S.: CataractNet: an automated cataract detection system using deep learning for fundus images. IEEE Access 9, 128799–128808 (2021)
11. Usha, R., Perumal, K.: SVM classification of brain images from MRI scans using morphological transformation and GLCM texture features. Int. J. Comput. Syst. Eng. 5(1), 18–23 (2019)
12. Junayed, M.S., Islam, M.B., Jeny, A.A., Sadeghzadeh, A., Biswas, T., Shah, A.F.M.S.: ScarNet: development and validation of a novel deep CNN model for acne scar classification with a new dataset. IEEE Access 10, 1245–1258 (2021)

13. Ansari, U.B., Sarode, T.: Skin cancer detection using image processing. Int. Res. J. Eng. Technol. **4**(4), 2875–2881 (2017)

14. Pham, T.-C., Luong, C.-M., Visani, M., Hoang, V.-D.: Deep CNN and data augmentation for skin lesion classification. In: Nguyen, N.T., Hoang, D.H., Hong, T.-P., Pham, H., Trawiński, B. (eds.) ACIIDS 2018. LNCS (LNAI), vol. 10752, pp. 573–582. Springer, Cham (2018). https://doi.org/10.1007/978-3-319-75420-8_54

15. Bhardwaj, A., Rege, P.P.: Skin lesion classification using deep learning. In: Merchant, S.N., Warhade, K., Adhikari, D. (eds.) Advances in Signal and Data Processing. LNEE, vol. 703, pp. 575–589. Springer, Singapore (2021). https://doi.org/10.1007/978-981-15-8391-9_42

16. Jianu, S.R.S., Ichim, L., Popescu, D.: Automatic diagnosis of skin cancer using neural networks. In: 2019 11th International Symposium on Advanced Topics in Electrical Engineering (ATEE), pp. 1–4. IEEE (2019)

17. Mengistu, A.D., Alemayehu, D.M.: Computer vision for skin cancer diagnosis and recognition using RBF and SOM. Int. J. Image Process. (IJIP) **9**(6), 311–319 (2015)

18. Barata, C., Figueiredo, M.A.T., Celebi, M.E., Marques, J.S.: Color identification in dermoscopy images using gaussian mixture models. In: 2014 IEEE International Conference on Acoustics, Speech and Signal Processing (ICASSP), pp. 3611–3615. IEEE (2014)

19. Mendonça, T., Ferreira, P.M., Marques, J.S., Marcal, A.R.S., Rozeira, J.: PH 2-a dermoscopic image database for research and benchmarking. In: 2013 35th Annual International Conference of the IEEE Engineering in Medicine and Biology Society (EMBC), pp. 5437–5440. IEEE (2013)

20. Misra, S., Wu, Y.: Machine learning assisted segmentation of scanning electron microscopy images of organic-rich shales with feature extraction and feature ranking. Gulf Professional Publishing (2020)

21. Liu, D., Yu, J.: Otsu method and k-means. In: 2009 Ninth International Conference on Hybrid Intelligent Systems, vol. 1, pp. 344–349. IEEE (2009)

22. Lee, S.U., Chung, S.Y., Park, R.H.: A comparative performance study of several global thresholding techniques for segmentation. Comput. Vis. Graph. Image Process. **52**(2), 171–190 (1990)

23. Isasi, A.G., Zapirain, B.G., Zorrilla, A.M.: Melanomas non-invasive diagnosis application based on the ABCD rule and pattern recognition image processing algorithms. Comput. Biol. Med. **41**(9), 742–755 (2011)

24. Thanh, D.N.H., Prasath, V.B.S., Hien, N.N., et al.: Melanoma skin cancer detection method based on adaptive principal curvature, colour normalisation and feature extraction with the ABCD rule. J. Digit. Imaging 1–12 (2019)

25. Garcia-Arroyo, J.L., Garcia-Zapirain, B.: Hypopigmentation pattern recognition in dermoscopy images for melanoma detection. J. Med. Imaging Health Inform. **5**(8), 1875–1879 (2015)

26. Chakravorty, R., Liang, S., Abedini, M., Garnavi, R.: Dermatologist-like feature extraction from skin lesion for improved asymmetry classification in PH 2 database. In: 2016 38th Annual International Conference of the IEEE Engineering in Medicine and Biology Society (EMBC), pp. 3855–3858. IEEE (2016)

27. Bi, L., Kim, J., Ahn, E., Feng, D., Fulham, M.: Automatic melanoma detection via multi-scale lesion-biased representation and joint reverse classification. In: 2016 IEEE 13th international symposium on biomedical imaging (ISBI), pp. 1055–1058. IEEE (2016)

28. Lattoofi, N.F., et al.: Melanoma skin cancer detection based on ABCD rule. In: 2019 First International Conference of Computer and Applied Sciences (CAS), pp. 154–157. IEEE (2019)

AI Used to Identify Car Accident Injury and Mortality Risk Factors in Dubai UAE

Asif Malik[✉] and Asad Safi[✉]

Department of Computing and Information Science, Higher Colleges of Technology,
Sharjah, UAE
{amalik,asafi}@hct.ac.ae

Abstract. There are several contributory risk factors that can cause road accidents in Dubai, UAE. This research examined systematically a range of relevant demographic, personality and attitudinal factors. Using AI, risk factors were identified that cause car accident in Dubai. Additionally, relevant connections of the relationship between gender and risky driving, and the relationship between perceived risk and risky driving are examined for each of the behaviors. The results demonstrate that the lists of significant predictors differed between risky driving behaviors. In addition, the perceived personal risk was observed to mediate the relationship between gender and age of the driver, and gender was observed to moderate the relationship between perceived risk and risky driving for drunk-driving and not wearing seat belts. The results highlight the importance of designing individual road safety interventions for individual driving behaviors and suggest factors that might be targeted in the younger driver population of Dubai.

Keywords: Machine learning · SAS Viya · Car accidents · Seat belt · Driver age · Risky driving

1 Introduction

The car driver's behavior on the road has been identified as a key contributor to road accidents [1]. Many people engage either in driving behaviors that are risky inadvertently or with the intention to "take the risk". Younger drivers are particularly partial to engage in risky driving [2]. Perhaps they tend to be inexperienced and lack the skills needed to negotiate difficult on-road driving situations, or have positive attitudes to taking risks by not wearing a seat belt.

Seat belt wearing was made compulsory in the United Arab Emirates (UAE) in January 1999 for drivers and front seat passengers only. On 1 July 2017, it became mandatory for all passengers to wear seat belts. In the United States of America, 48% of passengers died in car crashes were drivers and passengers that were not using seat belts [3]. With overall level of seat belt use in 2017 was at 90%. The remaining 10% accounts for almost half of all vehicle accidents deaths in the United States [4].

Public health and transportation professionals have agreed that seat belts are life-saving. However, strategies are needed to improve seat belt use among passengers and

© Springer Nature Switzerland AG 2022
C. Brito-Loeza et al. (Eds.): ISICS 2022, CCIS 1569, pp. 97–105, 2022.
https://doi.org/10.1007/978-3-030-98457-1_8

drivers. Some of the most effective population-based interventions have been the implementation of seat belt laws and the enhanced enforcement of such laws [4, 5] and [6]. These interventions have increased seat belt use and decreased crash related injuries and deaths. The seat belt laws have been very effective. These laws have been implemented by allowing police officers to stop vehicles and issue tickets when lack of seat belt use has been observed.

Seat belt usage has reached record levels in general with the execution of strategies such as those mentioned above. But some parts of the population continue to travel without seat belts. Dubai was the area of interest and was investigated in this research concerning seat belt usage. There were other factors that can identify individuals who would be prone to injury and mortality from a car accident. The main purpose of the current study was to investigate the risk factors of road car accident injury of road car accident and mortality rate in Dubai. The risk factors were investigated by using SAS Viya [10], which allowed the quick preparation of data and analysis using machine learning.

2 Literature Review

A key contributor to road accidents is risky driving behaviors, particularly for younger drivers [11]. Many studies have observed an association between several risky driving behaviors and road crashes, particularly for younger drivers. Speeding, not wearing seat belts, and driving whilst intoxicated (due to alcohol and/or drugs), are important risk related driving behaviors in terms of their contribution to road accidents. The Roads & Transport Authority Dubai estimated that, of all fatal crashes that occurred involved speeding or alcohol, the motor vehicle occupants were not wearing seat belts [12].

The review aims is to examine whether the pattern of relevant factors is different for the different behaviors. Past research [13], it has not been systematic in comparing the many factors related to the risky driving behaviors that are examined in the present research. Firstly, many studies have employed a general index of risky driving as the dependent variable [14], so results do not allow comparison of predictors across specific driving behaviors. Secondly, several factors have been investigated in relation to only one or two particular behaviors, but not in relation to other behaviors. A few studies have examined a full and parallel range of factors across several risky driving behaviors. For example, Begg et al. [15] investigated the factors associated with self-reported drunk-driving and driving after cannabis use and examined only a few predictive factors. The present study aimed to systematically examine a range of demographic factors, including the use of alcohol and recreational drugs and not wearing seat belts, via machine learning and AI. The present study considered factors that are specific to each behavior, as well as factors in general, framed in general terms, because recent studies have illustrated the importance of specific factors [16].

3   Methodology

A data set initially exclusively released by Dubai Police to SAS was used. The dataset consisted of 3179 traffic incidents in Dubai during 2017. The data set comprised of 19 attributes. The data dictionary is given below, in Table 1.

Table 1. Data dictionary

Attributes	Description
id	Record ID
psn_id	Driver ID, system generated
record_status	Status of record
acd_date	Date of accident
acd_time	Time of accident
acc_location	Location of accident
acc_type	Type of accident
acc_cause	Cause of accident
weather	Weather at the time of the accident
road_status	Road type
age	Age of driver
gender	Gender of driver
injury_severities	Severity of injury
driving_license_issue_date	Date the driving license was issued
Occupation	Occupation of the driver
Intoxication	If the driver was intoxicated
seat_belt_status	Seat belt or no seat belt
year_manufactured	Year of manufacture of the car
insurance_company_name	Name of the insurance company

The data recorded if there was no injury, injury or death. The category of injury was recorded as minor, moderate, severe or fatal. The data only identified trauma or death of the driver and did not identify whether passengers were also injured or died in the accident. Neither did the data identify how many of the car occupants suffered trauma or fatality.

There was some minor preprocessing of data with null values, filtering the tables, and categorizing accidents. A list of the categories for the cause of the accident is shown in Table 2.

The analysis was done using SAS Viya, a cloud-enabled, in-memory analytics engine. SAS Viya allowed quick data preparation for analytics using machine learning and AI suggestions.

Table 2. Accident cause category

Cause of accident	Description
Drugs/Medication	Driving under the influence of drugs, medication, alcohol, or a combination of these
Breaking traffic laws	Over speeding, trespassing, driving on the opposite side of the road, not keeping a safe distance between cars, driving recklessly, crashing into another vehicle, and running red lights
Not paying enough attention	Neglect, lack of attention, using a mobile phone, entering a road without checking for oncoming cars, opening a vehicle's door without paying attention, and not respecting other road users
Nature	Animals on the loose, poor weather and natural disasters
Negligence	Fatigue, drowsiness, sudden deviation, stopping in the middle of the road, wrong steering direction, backing up dangerously, not giving way
Vehicle related	Tire explosion, trailer detachment, vehicle loads falling, doors unlocked, outdated vehicle

4   Results and Discussion

To find a link between seat belt status (usage) and injury severity, the frequency of injury severity was grouped by seat belt status. The results showed that seat belt status affected the seriousness of the injury. Non-seat belt users scored a higher frequency in severe trauma and mortality than seat belt users. From Fig. 1, in accidents that resulted in death non-seat belt users had a 65% chance of dying as compared to seat belt users. In accidents that caused severe trauma non-seat belt users had a 66.7% chance of suffering severe trauma as compared to seat belt users. Out of all the accidents that occurred in 2017 that resulted in injury or death, 4.8% of non-seat belt users died compared to 2.6% of seat belt users. If an accident is likely to involve injury non-seat users are twice as likely to die as compared to a seat belt user.

It can also be derived that 58.5% of all accidents involved injury also involved non-seat belt users. This is only marginally more than accidents that involved seat belt users.

Interestingly, seat belt users recorded a higher frequency in both minor to moderate injuries, than seat belt nonusers, Fig. 1.

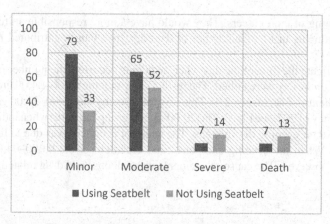

Fig. 1. Frequency of trauma type by seat belt statu

This higher rate of minor and moderate injuries in seat belt users is not connected with seat belt usage but more with driving skills.

Next, identifying the age groups with the most accidents was analyzed.

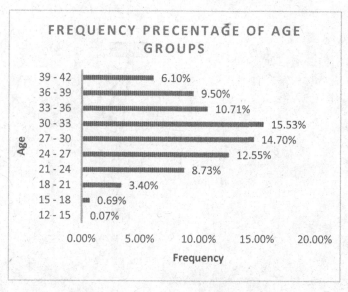

Fig. 2. Frequency percentage of age groups.

The ages were divided into groups with a range of three years, starting from the age of 12 to the age of 80. Figure 2 identified the frequency of accidents based on the age groups began to gradually increase from the age of 18 reaching to its highest in the age bracket of 30 to 33. The frequency of accidents then slowly starts to decrease. Age groups that scored 10% or more of the accidents were 24–27, 27-30, 30–36 and 33–36.Ordinarily, individuals in their late twenties would be married to a young family at the beginning of their careers. They would have a more responsible attitude to fulfil their commitments in life. This is not observed, which can be attributed to the local culture.

To investigate the time of the day when accidents occurred, the number of accidents in each hour of the day were tallied. The results show that the 03:00–04:00 group had the highest frequency of accidents, 210. This was followed by the 20:00–21:00 group which had a frequency of 207, see Fig. 3. The 20:00–21:00 group indicates when individuals are going out to their evening destinations. The cause of accidents was due to the breaking traffic laws. When the evening ends bars, and clubs close, the 03:00–04:00 spike in accidents is observed. The cause of accidents were alcohol and drug related.

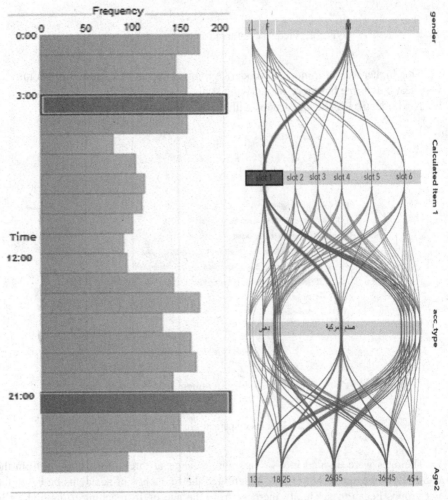

Fig. 3. Frequency of accidents againt time.   **Fig. 4.** Parallel coordinates showing relationship with selected variables.

An analysis was done using parallel coordinates on selected variables that were of interest: time,the cause of accidents, age, gender, seat belt status and trauma severity. The results are shown in Fig. 4. Time was broken down into six slots. Where slots that became of interest after inspecting the results were slot one which was from 03:00–04:00, and slot six,which was 20:00–21:00.

From the analysis, two distinct categories can be identified. The first category is a specific group with accidents in time slot six (20:00–21:00). The leading cause of traffic accidents was due to breaking traffic laws, and the age group was between the ages of 18 to 25 years of age. Males dominated this category, most of them had seat belts on, which led to minor injuries.

The second category was a distinct group reported to have accidents occurring in time slot one (03:00–04:00). The main cause of traffic accidents was due to alcohol, recreational drugs and medication. This category had individuals between the ages of 26 to 35 years. Males also dominated this category, most of them had seat belts on,which led to minor injuries.

To further investigate seat belt status and the usage of drugs (recreational and medication)and alcohol, another parallel coordinates analysis was done, Fig. 5. It is apparent

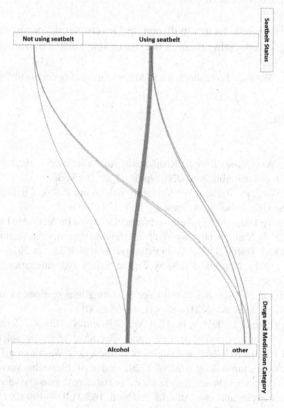

Fig. 5. Parallel coordinates for seat belt status and drugs and alcohol.

that although individuals were using seat belts, they were driving under the influence of either drugs, alcohol or both. Further, Fig. 5 shows that alcohol consumption plays a more important role than the usage of drugs and medication in causing road accidents. It should be noted that drivers under the influence of alcohol tend to use their seat belts. This could be that the driver is aware that they are under the influence of alcohol and are taking precautions by wearing a seat belt.

5 Conclusion

This work has identified that there are a number of risk factors that can be used to identify drivers that are likely to cause a traffic accident. The severity of injury and the mortality rate are affected by the usage of seat belts. The critical identifying risk factors amongst Dubai car drivers include being:

- Male.
- 24–36 years of age. This age group scored 10% or more of the accidents.
- Driving between 20:00–21:00 and 03:00–04:00.
- Using alcohol, drugs, or both.

These identifying risk factors will enable Governmental departments to suitably target such groups in educating them in the use of seat belts and driving safely.

Acknowledgment. We would like thank SAS (MENA) for giving access to SAS Viya.

References

1. Australian Transport Safety Bureau. Road deaths Australia: 2015 statistical summary (2016). http://www.atsb.gov.au/publications/2016/pdf/rda_ss_2015.pdf
2. Clarke, D.D., Ward, P., Truman, W.: Voluntary risk taking and skill deficits in young driver accidents in the UK. Accid. Anal. Prev. **37**, 523–529 (2005)
3. National Highway Traffic Safety Administration. Occupant Protection in Passenger Vehicles. (DOT HS 812 374). National Highway Traffic Safety Administration, Washington, DC (2017)
4. National Highway Traffic Safety Administration. Seat Belt Use in 2016—Overall Results. (DOT HS 812 351). National Highway Traffic Safety Administration, Washington, DC (2016a)
5. Dinh-Zarr, T.B., et al.: Reviews of evidence regarding interventions to increase the use of safety belts. Am. J. Prev. Med. **21**(4 Suppl), 48–65 (2001)
6. Goodwin, A., Thomas, L., Kirley, B., Hall, W., O'Brien, N., Hill, K.: Countermeasures That Work: Highway Safety Countermeasure Guide For State Highway Safety Offices Eighth Edition. (DOT HS 812 202). National Highway Traffic Safety, Washington, DC (2015). https://www.nhtsa.gov/sites/nhtsa.dot.gov/files/812202-countermeasuresthatwork8th.pdf
7. Lee, L.K., et al.: Motor vehicle crash fatalities in states with primary versus secondary seat belt laws: a time-series analysis. Ann. Intern. Med. **163**(3), 184–190 (2015). https://doi.org/10.7326/m14-2368

8. Beck, L.F., Downs, J., Stevens, M.R., Sauber-Schatz, E.K.: Rural and urban differences in passenger-vehicle-occupant deaths and seat belt use among adults – United States, 2014. MMWR Surveill. Summ. **66**(17), 1–13 (2017). https://doi.org/10.15585/mmwr.ss6617a1
9. Strine, T.W., Beck, L.F., Bolen, J., Okoro, C., Dhingra, S., Balluz, L.: Geographic and sociodemographic variation in self-reported seat belt use in the United States. Accid. Anal. Prevent. **42**(4), 1066–1071 (2010). https://doi.org/10.1016/j.aap.2009.12.014
10. About the SAS. https://www.sas.com/en_us/company-information.html#history. Accessed September 2020
11. Turner, C., McClure, R., Pirozzo, S.: Injury and risk-taking behaviour – a systematic review. Accid. Anal. Prev. **36**(1), 93–101 (2014)
12. RTA Dubai. https://traffic.rta.ae/
13. Yagil, D.: Beliefs, motives and situational factors related to pedestrians' self-reported behavior at signal-controlled crossings. Transp. Res. Part F **3**, 1–13 (2017)
14. Dahlen, E.R., Martin, R.C., Ragan, K., Kuhlman, M.M.: Driving anger, sensation seeking, impulsiveness, and boredom proneness in the prediction of unsafe driving. Accid. Anal. Prev. **37**, 341–348 (2005)
15. Begg, D.J., Langley, J.D., Stephenson, S.: Identifying factors that predict persistent driving after drinking, unsafe driving after drinking, and driving after using cannabis among young adults. Accid. Anal. Prev. **35**, 669–675 (2003)
16. Fernandes, R., Job, R.F.S., Hatfield, J.: Different factors predict different risky driving behaviours: a challenge to the assumed generalizability of prediction and countermeasure. J. Saf. Res. **38**(1), 59–70 (2017)

Toward Automatic Water Pollution Analysis: A Machine Learning Approach for Water-Quality Monitoring Through Pattern Classification of Water Crystallization

Lavdie Rada[1]([⊠])(ⓘ), Yusuf Baran Tanrıverdi[1], Ömer Ekmel Kara[1], Elizabeth M. Hemond[1], and Ulaş Tezel[2]

[1] Bahçeşehir University, 34349 Beşiktaş, İstanbul, Turkey
lavdie.rada@eng.bau.edu.tr
[2] Boğaziçi University, Beşiktaş, İstanbul, Turkey

Abstract. Heavy metal contamination in drinking water and water resources is one of the problems generated by increasing water demand and growing industrialization. Heavy metals can be toxic to humans and other living beings when their intake surpasses a certain threshold. Generally, heavy metal contamination analysis of water resources requires qualified experts with specialized equipment. In this paper, we introduce a method for citizen-based water-quality monitoring through simple pattern classification of water crystallization using a smartphone and portable microscope. This work is a first step toward the development of a Water Expert System smartphone application that will provide the ability to analyze water resource contamination remotely by sending images to the database and receiving an automatic analysis of the sample via machine learning software. In this study, we show the ability of the method to detect Fe 2 mg/1 L, 5 mg/L, 10 mg/L polluted distilled water compared with other heavy metals (Al, Pb) pollution. The experimental results show that the classification used method has an accuracy greater than 90%.

Keywords: Water pollution · Convolutional Neuron Network (CNN) · Visual Geometry Group (VGG) · U-net · Classification

1 Introduction

Improving access to clean water for people around the world requires knowledge about sources of contamination and the ability to detect chemical contaminants. Most individuals routinely using a given water source do not have quick and easy methods available to detect contamination; instead, laboratory work, expensive equipment, and specialized experts are required. One of the main issues with water pollution is the presence of heavy metals [1]. Heavy metals are metals that have higher atomic weight than sodium (e.g., iron, aluminum, mercury, lead, etc.,), (Brewer, 1983) [2]. They can be bio-accumulated

This project was partially supported by BAUBAP 2019.01.05.

through the food chain and can be toxic even at low concentrations (EPA, 2000) [3]. Heavy metals in the water can be analyzed in detail by several atomic spectrometry-based devices like FAAS, GAAS, ICP-OES, ICP-MS [1]. These devices require a facility and qualified person to operate them and cannot be conducted on the field. The study of Zhong et al. [4] suggests that dried patterns of different nanoparticles from different materials show repetitive patterns. If these patterns can be found to be repetitive in the same species and concentration of heavy metals in water, machine learning algorithms can be developed to recognize these patterns. Our study aims to develop a method to detect water contamination easily and cheaply, using an application that can be run on a personal smartphone. In this research, we propose to use the 'pollution crystal formation effect', produced by dissolved minerals and chemicals after the water evaporates, to analyze pollution components in a single drop of water. This new study and its output software will allow the general public to test the quality of their tap water and have a water quality pre-examination by simply uploading a photo of an air-dried water droplet taken from a smartphone. In this study, the possibility of creating a pre-analysis method that requires only a machine learning algorithm and portable microscopes (60X) to identify certain heavy metals in certain concentrations was investigated. The first dataset obtained for such experiments contains dried droplets from different resources and 3 heavy metals Al, Fe, Pb in different percentages were formed for investigation of detection in diluted water. The data shown in this paper is collected in the Chemistry Lab. of Bahçeşehir University. More data of combined elements and tap water from different cities of Turkey as well as from different cities in the world is in an ongoing process. This study consists of three heavy metals as water pollution. Our ongoing data collection consists of combined heavy metals investigated in lab conditions as well as tap water images analyzed for different contaminations. The first step of our future work consists of studying the repetitive patterns in different combinations followed by the applications of this methodology. The second step will engage the collection of different tap waters and naturally occurring or artificially generated waters polluted with heavy metals patterns. Short term aim of this study is to demonstrate that single-type heavy metals can be distinguished from each other in distilled water with the help of hybrid Machine Learning models. More details can be found in Sect. 2. Hybrid machine learning techniques that have been applied to detect Fe 2 mg/L, 5 mg/L, and 10 mg/L polluted water against other sources of heavy-metal pollution, such as Al and Pb, are explained in Sect. 3. Different experiment settings are explained in Sect. 4. Overall, it is seen to using a pre-trained ANN to feed ML algorithm has contributed to the robustness of classification.

2   Dataset Collection

As the first stage of our research, we set a proper method of water sample preparation for the image analysis of retaining material after evaporation. In the following, we detail the materials used, sample preparation protocol, and image acquisition of the data. The materials used for the data collection include Carson MicroBrite Plus 60x–120x LED Lighted Pocket Microscope, Plexi plates, 1–10 μL Micropipette, iPhone X camera, $PbCl_2$, $FeCl_2.4H_2O$, $AlCl_3.6H_2O$. Three Heavy Metals (Fe, Pb, Al) were chosen for the initial phase of the study. The metal resources used are $FeCl_2.4H_2O$, $PbCl_2$, and

$AlCl_3.6H_2O$. These compounds were dissolved in diluted water as instructed in the following protocol:

Materials and Items

$AlCl_3.6H_2O$ powder (MW: 241.43 g/mol, water solubility: 50 mg/mL), 100-mL HNO_3 acid-washed glass volumetric flask or plastic volumetric flask, 1 mL pipette tips 100-mL HNO_3 acid-washed glass volumetric flask or plastic volumetric flask, 1 mL pipette tips, 100 µL pipette tips, Pipettors, Teflon coated mixing-rods, Paper, or plastic weighing dish.

2.1 Procedure

Preparation of 200 mg Al_3+/L Stock Solution

1. Weigh **179 mg** (or **0.179 g** as it appears on the scale) $AlCl_3.6H_2O$ (MW Al^{3+} = 26.98 g/mole, to get 1 gr Al^{3+} one has to use 8.95 g $AlCl_3.6H_2O$.:::: $MWAlCl_3.6H_2O/MWAl^{3+}$).
2. Add some DI water (50–75 mL) into a 100-mL volumetric flask containing a Teflon-coated mixing rod.
3. Add already weighed 179 mg $AlCl_3.6H_2O$ into the volumetric flask containing some DI water (step 2).
4. Let the powder dissolve in the water while the whole content is agitated on a stirrer.
5. Take the mixing rod out.
6. Make the volume to 100 mL, shake the flask, and transfer the content into a plastic storage bottle.

Preparation of Spiked Water Samples

Caution 1: All samples should be prepared with real drinking water that you choose to work with. It can be bottled water or tap water. Samples prepared with DI water may be used as a control, and non-spiked water can be used as a reference.

Caution 2: Every concentration must be prepared in a different flask. If you are going to use the same flask for the preparation of different solutions, then you must wash it with a dilute nitric acid solution (0.02N) to avoid cross-contamination.

1. 50–75 mL water was added into a 100-mL volumetric flask containing a Teflon coated mixing rod.
2. **1 mL** stock Al^{3+} added solution described above to prepare **2 mg Al^{3+}/L** working solution.
3. Make the volume to 100 mL, shake the flask and transfer the contents into a plastic storage bottle.

The amount of stock solution that you need to use for other spiked samples is given below (Table 1):

Table 1. The necessary amount of stock solution per spiked samples

Spike concentration (mg/L)	The volume of stock solution (mL)
2.0	1.000
0.5	0.250
0.2	0.100
0.1	0.050

Based on Turkish and WHO drinking water standards the concentrations for Al^{3+} defined based on 0.1, **0.2** [TSE Limit], 0.5, 2.0 mg Al^{3+}/L. Same for **Fe**: 0.1, **0.2** [TSE Limit], 1.0, 2.0 mg Fe/L **Pb**: 0.005, **0.01** [TSE Limit], 0.05, 0.1 mg Pb/L.

For consistency, in this work, we show only the photos taken with an iPhone. We acknowledge that there is a high similarity for other phones used to take the picture of our experiments.

2.2 Used Concentrations

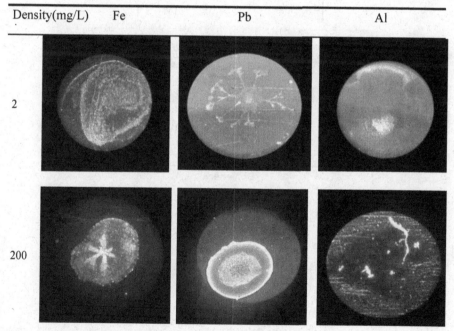

Density(mg/L)	Fe	Pb	Al
2			
200			

Fig. 1. Dataset samples: images of two different concentration densities of each of the three elements (Fe, Pb, Al) investigated.

To enlarge the number of samples different concentrations were considered to determine the significance of the patterns resulting from dried droplets. $FeCl_2.4H_2O$, $PbCl_2$, and $AlCl_3.6H_2O$ were used as metal resources. These compounds were solved in diluted water as was instructed in the Protocol. 179 mg $AlCL_3.6H_2O$, 331 mg $FeCl_2.4H_2O$, and 268,44 mg $PbCl_2$, each was solved in 100 ml of diluted water by stirring on stirrer with fish for 1 min to generate 200 mg/1L stock solutions for each of three metals and then used for further generation of samples with different concentrations. Different 100 ml flasks were used for each sample preparation. 200 mg/L and 2 mg/L of Al and Pb solutions and 20 mg/L, 10 mg/L, 5 mg/L, 2 mg/L of Fe solutions were generated by diluting stock solution in diluted water, for the sample collection of the initial phase of this study. 1 µL of each prepared sample taken with a micropipette (1–10 µL) and dropped onto Plexi plates and left to dry till it's fully dried which usually takes 3 to 6 h.

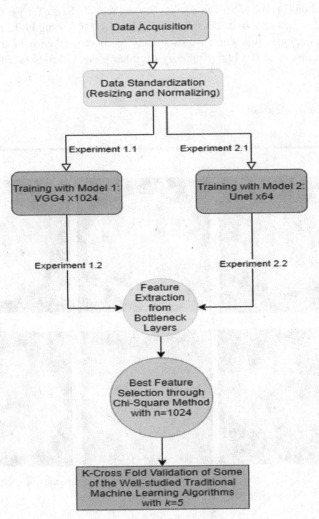

Fig. 2. Workflow of our study

2.3 Image Acquisition

The images of dried droplets of samples with different concentrations of 3 types of metals on plexi plates were acquired with 60x objective in an optical microscope (Carson MicroBrite Plus 60x–120x LED Lighted Pocket Microscope) with an iPhone X cell phone camera of 12 megapixels. 50–60 Images for each concentration of 3 metal solutions were stored in jpeg format in files with names that indicate types of water and metal with their concentration and other variables such as its magnification. The experimental images are shown in Fig. 1.

3 Methodology

Figure 2 shows the workflow of the study.

3.1 Challenges of Small Datasets: Overfitting

The most challenging problem with limited datasets is the risk of overfitting the machine learning model, named the 'bugbear of machine learning [5]. Chicco et al. [6] state the reason behind the occurrence of overfitting is that the model is designed to solve two problems together: in the training phase, it must decrease its performance error to a minimum level, yet during validation, the need is that correct predictions or *scores specified in compilation* must be maximized on unseen data. This duality may cause a performance drop through the next epochs' validation phase while the model still 'memorizes' the data in the training phase. As it is suggested, this is more likely to happen when the amount of data samples is very few. In those cases, every hyperparameter must be considered carefully. For example, if the 'depth' or complexity of the neural network is exceeding some level, the possibility of overfitting is increasing [7]. Fortunately, changing model architecture by adding regularizing layers such as L1/L2 regularization, dropout layers, or removing some of the extent layers [7] can be a solution other than largening the dataset, if not possible. In some cases, rather than changing built-in models, more practical solutions can be introduced such as setting an early callback [7]. Although, this can give no benefits if the model tends to overfit quickly due to obvious reasons (small dataset, excessive noise), as it would result in a non-optimized result in the trade-off of the epoch numbers and performance. Hinton et al. [8] study the great effectiveness of dropout layers, concerning error rate on the test/validation phase and report that this process can be seen as a very efficient way of averaging neural networks. The principle of dropout layers works as dropping currently hidden units with a probability of a previously chosen rate, generally 0.5 or 0.3. In our study, we tried to handle overfitting by adding dropout layers after the fully connected layers of the CNN.

3.2 Proposed Models

At present, the number of works on CNNs is humungous considering there are lots of architectures, layer types invented, and optimizations for each data type that can be set differently therefore research continues. One of the research points is whether to create a hybrid model that consists of an ANN or CNN specifically in Image Classification, as feature extractor and a conventional ML method as classifier head, instead of a couple of Fully Connected Layer. The idea of CNNs to be used as feature extractors and considering the selected *best n*-features for other machine learning algorithms is not new, several research productions such as [11, 12], and [13] have done this process to achieve better results in classification purposes. The two proposed models of CNN are trained to classify sample images, to be used as a feature extractor for the next step where traditional machine learning algorithms listed in Tables are used for final classification.

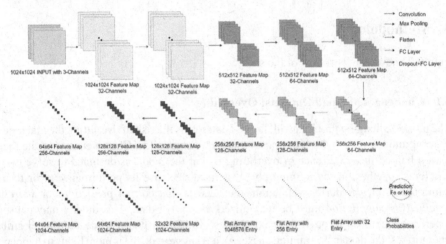

Fig. 3. VGG-5 model architecture

VGG-5. VGGNet is a neural network first configured by Visual Geometry Group (VGG), introduced by Simonyan et al. [9]. The structure of a VGG block is the stack of a number (in general, 2) of convolutional layers with one max pooling layer at the end of the block. Despite more deep architectures being used, we work with a simple 5-block VGG to avoid overfitting and it would be surprisingly sufficient assuming image patterns are very distinguishable, and the dataset is clean. As classification head, we use three fully connected layers where each dropout layer is put ahead. Figure 3 shows our model architecture.

U-Net: A Biomedical Focused Deep Learning Model. Created for segmentation purposes, U-Net gives a good insight into the features of an image [10]. We add a classification head that consists of three fully connected layers and two dropout layers between each of them. Figure 4 shows our U-Net model architecture. The double convolution layers are merged into one in the figure for easy follow. Note that, the bottleneck layer is where the smallest and many features are extracted where through up-sampling segmentation occurs. The classification head remains the same structure as VGG-5 with appropriate numbers.

3.3   Feature Extraction

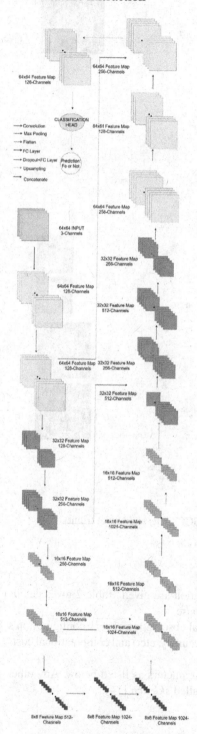

Fig. 4. U-Net model architecture

To extract the features of samples, an intermediate layer is selected as the pivot the last point from the model. Ideally, any convolutional layer from the architecture may be used, and then adding a flattening layer would produce you a 1D array feature list. In our study, for the first two models, we used the next to last layer approach and removed the FC layers for advanced fitting. For U-Net, the bottleneck layer, the layer before the up-sampling starts might be more appropriate since the original purpose of this model of mask creation is not our focus. Thus, pre-trained U-Net's bottleneck features were obtained to see the results by an advanced fitting of the machine learning algorithm. Figure 5 shows some piece-wise generated features from models for better visualization of human-eye.

3.4   Feature Selection

For feature selection, the Chi-square method is chosen to grab the best relevant n features via the library *sklearn*'s function having all scores for each feature, we limit the amount to some n number to have the best scores, i.e., the most relevant ones. The *number* for all experiments is chosen as 1024, as the number of features is very large after flattening the output of segmentation heads.

3.5   Machine Learning Classifiers

For this study, we use the seven most common algorithms which for each we applied a k-Fold Cross-Validation. These methods are listed in Tables with a comparison of results. For general application, k is chosen as 5.

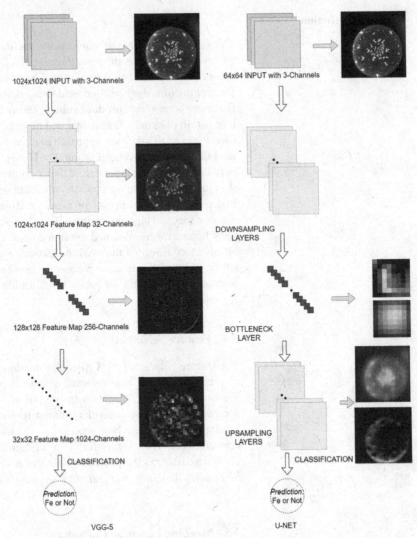

Fig. 5. Features extraction samples from VGG-5 (left) and U-Net (right).

4   Implementation and Results

In the following, more details on the parameterization are given. Table 2 gives details on the used hyperparameters during the training phase.

The hyperparameters are chosen by experimental observation of each configuration's performance rise in validation phase scores (loss, accuracy, etc.) and computational costs (memory, runtime).

Some of the classifier tools used have fixed parameters as listed below. Any other parameters are set to default by a Python library called *sklearn* [14].

Table 2. Hyperparameters of the proposed experiments

	U-net model	VGG5 model
Batch size	10	5
Number of epochs	25	25
Learning rate	0.001	0.0001
Momentum	0.9	0.9
Dropout rate	0.3	0.3
Activation function	Softmax	Softmax
Optimizer model	Adam	SGD
Input size	128	128
Loss function	Categorical cross-entropy	Categorical cross-entropy

Extra Trees Classifier: Number of the parallel processors in the tress is 4. The number of trees is set to 100. The function to measure the quality of a split is chosen as '*gini*'. The minimum number of samples needed to split a node is 10. The maximum depth of the tree is 40 while the minimum number of samples needed to be leaf node is 4.

Random Forest Classifier: Number of the parallel processors in the tress is 4. The number of trees is set to 70. The function to measure the quality of a split is chosen as '*entropy*', The minimum number of samples needed to split a node is 5.

K-Neighbors Classifier: Number of parallel processors is 4. Only one K-Neighbor is used.

The experiments are done using *TensorFlow* and *Keras* Framework in *Python* on Virtual Desktops with 64 GB RAM and Intel R Platinum 8272CL 2.59 GHz CPU provided by Bahcesehir University. Each model training consumed an amount of memory in RAM between 40%–62.5%. The training phases of VGG-5 and U-Net last about 10 min and 45 min respectively for $128 \times 128 \times 3$ images.

4.1 Experiment 1

In this experiment, the comparison is made between samples crystallized with **2 mg Fe and the other non-Fe crystallized sample**. The results of the automatic identification process of heavy metals scanned through the different used architectures are shown in Table 3. The U-Net model trained on data was able to perform better compared to VGG-5, in general. However, one may observe in Fig. 6 easily the phenomena called overfitting occurred with U-Net. The scores were not perfect for the test and validation sets despite outputting %100 accuracies during the training phase, indicating overfitting. Noting that, since the validation and test dataset is only 20% of the dataset, the probability of false 'perfect classification' has been increased for both CNN models. As supported by the graphics of Fig. 6, unsurprisingly by the time model learns from the training dataset, it already fits on the validation dataset, therefore creating an illusion of learning resulting in a performance drop on unseen data. VGG seems to be more reliable in evaluation in terms of validation scores following training scores, yet the performance is doubtful enough again as we cannot rely on small test datasets. Despite these reliability issues, these experiments show that with a huge dataset in the future, it is possible to detect element crystallization in high confidence.

Table 3. Scores of the base models for distinguishing the water samples crystallized with 2 mg Fe and non-Fe elements.

Models	Evaluation scores			Train phases' scores			Validation phases' scores		
	Accuracy	F1 score	ROC-AUC score	Accuracy	F1 score	ROC-AUC score	Accuracy	F1 score	ROC-AUC score
U-Net	**0.9487**	**0.9473**	**0.9974**	1	1	1	0.8750	0.8770	0.8906
VGG-5	0.7949	0.8027	0.9402	0.9140	0.9137	0.9705	0.8333	0.8357	0.9661

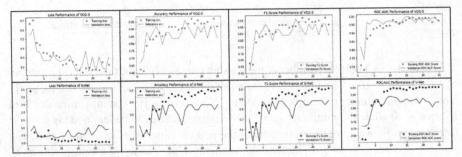

Fig. 6. Performance of two base models for distinguishing the water samples crystallized with 2 mg Fe and non-Fe elements.

To have better and more reliable outputs, the features of every sample (no split as train or test) from our dataset is mapped with, firstly, the last layer before a dense layer of pretrained VGG-5, later bottleneck layer of the U-Net (See Fig. 5 for visualization). After the procedure of eliminating less relevant features through the Chi-Square method, Machine learning methods are applied on every 500 features from both models now with parameters of several cross-fold (k) equals 10. The results for each model are given in Tables 4 and 5. We see, Linear Discriminant Analysis fit on features from classical CNN seemed to outnumber other models and base models in both Accuracy and F-score and results in almost %100 ROC-AUC, while SVM reaches this maximum level. Most of the models pass the base VGG-5 model in metrics (blue marked) except QDA while, U-Net Bottleneck features have not shown any improvement.

This huge increment in performance shows that indeed features can be beneficial to extend the classification process to reach higher levels. For the models fit on pretrained U-Net bottleneck features, however, that improvement is not the case. We may say, SVM, LDA, and Random Forest Classifier's output higher than 90% accuracy indicate success and may give better results in real-life applications.

4.2 Experiment 2

In this experiment we collected **5 and 10 mg Iron samples, to teach our models to distinguish them from 2 mg Al & Pb.** The goal is to see if the pattern can be detectable

Table 4. Scores of Hybrid models with VGG-5 base for distinguishing the water samples crystallized with 2 mg Fe and non-Fe elements.

Fit with features from pre-trained VGG-5	Accuracy	F1 score	ROC-AUC score
Linear support vector machine	0.987 (0.026)	0.987 (0.027)	**1.0 (0.0)**
Linear discriminant	**0.993 (0.020)**	**0.993 (0.020)**	0.998 (0.005)
Quadratic discriminant	0.681 (0.132)	0.466 (0.218)	0.673 (0.172)
Gaussian naïve bayes	0.960 (0.080)	0.959 (0.085)	0.967 (0.062)
Random tress	0.980 (0.030)	0.984 (0.032)	0.990 (0.024)
Extra trees	0.980 (0.030)	0.971 (0.052)	0.994 (0.012)
K-nearest neighbor	0.981 (0.040)	0.982 (0.037)	0.981 (0.041)

Table 5. Scores of Hybrid models with U-Net base for distinguishing the water samples crystallized with 2 mg Fe and non-Fe elements.

Fit with features from pre-trained U-Net	Accuracy	F1 score	ROC-AUC score
Linear SVM	0.904 (0.057)	0.854 (0.118)	0.965 (0.037)
Linear discriminant	0.915 (0.089)	0.883 (0.116)	0.959 (0.060)
Quadratic discriminant	0.635 (0.093)	0.086 (0.175)	0.894 (0.050)
Gaussian Naïve Bayes	0.873 (0.068)	0.835 (0.135)	0.896 (0.051)
Random tress	0.904 (0.058)	0.876 (0.128)	0.971 (0.035)
Extra trees	0.872 (0.062)	0.784 (0.194)	0.935 (0.062)
K-nearest neighbor	0.833 (0.060)	0.787 (0.080)	0.830 (0.057)

even from a mix of differently densified water samples. Although they have similar results seen in Table 6, VGG-5 seems to have good approximations on the data, and it is observed in Fig. 7 as well.

Table 6. Scores of Base models for Experiment 2: Distinguishing water samples crystallized with 5 and 10 mg Fe from others crystallized with 2 mg Al or Pb.

Models	Evaluation scores			Train phases' scores			Validation phases' scores		
	Accuracy	F1 score	ROC-AUC score	Accuracy	F1 score	ROC-AUC score	Accuracy	F1 score	ROC-AUC score
U-Net	0.8298	0.8282	0.9013	**0.9369**	0.9369	0.9709	0.7857	0.7846	0.8584
VGG-5	**0.9149**	**0.9114**	**0.9846**	**0.9369**	**0.9372**	**0.9728**	**0.8571**	**0.8488**	**0.9605**

Following the same procedure (number of cross folds, $k = 10$ and number of best features, $n = 500$), once again CNN networks are used to train traditional algorithms, to detect any behavioral differentiation from previous experimentations. As shown in Table 7, repeatedly SVM and LDA have shown progress along with the K-Nearest Neighbor Algorithm. The increments concerning the base model (blue marks) are around %1–5 for

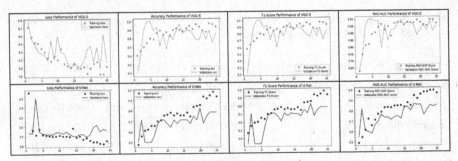

Fig. 7. Performance of two base models for distinguishing the water samples crystallized with 5 mg and 10 mg Fe and non-Fe elements consisting of 2 mg AI or Pb.

accuracy and F1-score while ROC-AUC score almost reached out perfect classification through LDA, SVM, and Extra Trees methods. Consistent with the other outputs, U-Net has not shown significant advancement in this one except for minimal increments in Accuracy and ROC-AUC scores (Table 8).

Table 7. Scores of Hybrid models with VGG-5 base for distinguishing the water samples crystallized with 5 mg and 10 mg Fe and non-Fe elements consisting of 2 mg AI or Pb.

Fit with features from pre-trained VGG-5	Accuracy	F1 score	ROC-AUC score
Linear support vector machine	0.951 (0.045)	**0.948 (0.049)**	0.993 (0.011)
Linear discriminant	0.951 (0.038)	0.945 (0.041)	**0.995 (0.012)**
Quadratic discriminant	0.504 (0.131)	0.636 (0.113)	0.761 (0.155)
Gaussian Naïve Bayes	0.936 (0.066)	0.926 (0.072)	0.948 (0.049)
Random tress	0.936 (0.052)	0.937 (0.053)	0.989 (0.013)
Extra trees	0.952 (0.044)	0.930 (0.058)	0.992 (0.012)
K-nearest neighbor	**0.962 (0.035)**	0.948 (0.071)	0.959 (0.047)

Table 8. Scores of Hybrid models with U-Net base for distinguishing the water samples crystallized with 5 mg and 10 mg Fe and non-Fe elements consisting of 2 mg AI or Pb.

Fit with features from pre-trained U-Net	Accuracy	F1 score	ROC-AUC score
Linear SVM	0.775 (0.107)	0.754 (0.139)	0.880 (0.096)
Linear discriminant	**0.842 (0.062)**	0.721 (0.081)	0.752 (0.077)
Quadratic discriminant	0.648 (0.109)	0.613 (0.133)	0.726 (0.138)
Gaussian Naïve Bayes	0.802 (0.090)	0.785 (0.112)	0.837 (0.104)
Random tress	0.817 (0.085)	0.800 (0.122)	0.902 (0.061)
Extra trees	0.833 (0.078)	**0.802 (0.125)**	**0.904 (0.051)**
K-nearest neighbor	0.796 (0.069)	0.761 (0.117)	0.797 (0.079)

5 Conclusion and Future Remarks

In this study, we showed some preliminary results on the Fe water polluted data and automatic detection of such pollution. The results obtained indicate the appropriateness of the method for further investigation on other similar heavy metal polluted samples. We acknowledge that this study is in its early stage. Our group is working on a full set of data collection. More data with combined polluted agents and data collected from real tap water in different cities are in the early stage of its collection. Figure 8 shows the images of the tap water collected from NY city and Boston in the USA. We see different patterns in each of them which directly relates to the type of agent contaminating the water. Concerning the improvement of the effectiveness of the proposed models, more data is required. Another great challenge in this kind of study is ground-truthing the water composition annotation for tap-water samples. This work is the first step toward an automated tool that can avoid long labor work in labs and is easily used by anyone that follows a certain instruction. The team is working on data collection and annotation which will be soon provided for research purposes. After the data collection is completed there will be two additional problems to resolve in the water ring classification task: different density detection and multiple pollution classification.

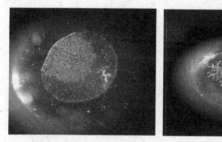

Fig. 8. Water pollution for NY City (left) and Boston USA

References

1. Adverse health effects of heavy metals in children. World Health Organization (2011)
2. Brewer, M., Scott, T. (eds.): Concise Encyclopedia of Biochemistry. Walter de Gruyter, Berlin, New York (1983)
3. Poyraz, B.: Farklı Lokasyonlardan Alınan İçme Sularında Ağır Metal Analizi [The heavy metal analysis of drinking waters sampled from different locations]. University of Düzce, Bilim ve Teknoloji Dergisi, no. 2 (2014)
4. Zhong, X., Xie, H., Duan, F.: Deposition patterns from evaporating sessile droplets with suspended mixtures of multi-sized and multi-species hydrophilic and non-adsorbing nanoparticles. Appl. Therm. Eng. **111**, 1565–1572 (2017)
5. Domingos, P.: A few useful things to know about machine learning. Commun ACM. **55**(10), 78–87 (2012). https://doi.org/10.1145/2347736.2347755
6. Chicco, D.: Ten quick tips for machine learning in computational biology. BioData Min. **10**(35), 8 (2017). https://doi.org/10.1186/s13040-017-0155-3

7. Ying, X.: An overview of overfitting and its solutions. J. Phys. Conf. Ser. **1168**, 022022 (2019)
8. Hinton, G., Srivastava, N., Krizhevsky, A., Sutskever, I., Salakhutdinov, R.: Improving neural networks by preventing co-adaptation of feature detectors. arXiv preprint arXiv:1207.0580 (2012)
9. Simonyan, K., Zisserman, A.: Very deep convolutional networks for large-scale image recognition. arXiv preprint arXiv:1409.1556 (2014)
10. Ronneberger, O., Fischer, P., Brox, T.: U-net: convolutional networks for biomedical image segmentation. arXiv:1505.04597 (2015)
11. Simon, P., Vijayasundaram, U.: Deep learning-based feature extraction for texture classification. Proc. Comput. Sci. **171**, 1680–1687 (2020). https://doi.org/10.1016/j.procs.2020.04.180
12. Razavian, A.S., et al.: CNN features off-the-shelf: an astounding baseline for recognition. In: 2014 IEEE Conference on Computer Vision and Pattern Recognition Workshops, pp. 512–519 (2014)
13. Petrovska, B., Zdravevski, E., Lameski, P., Corizzo, R., Štajduhar, I., Lerga, J.: Deep learning for feature extraction in remote sensing: a case-study of aerial scene classification. Sensors **20**, 3906 (2020). https://doi.org/10.3390/s20143906
14. https://scikit-learn.org/stable/modules/classes.html#module-sklearn.ensemble. Accessed 29 Oct 2021

Evaluation of Human Pose Estimation in 3D with Monocular Camera for Clinical Application

José Carrasco-Plaza[1,2,3(✉)] and Mauricio Cerda[1,2]

[1] SCIAN-Lab, Programa de Biología Integrativa, Instituto de Ciencias Biomédicas, Facultad de Medicina, Universidad de Chile, Santiago, Chile
[2] Centro de Informática Médica y Telemedicina, Facultad de Medicina, Universidad de Chile, Santiago, Chile
[3] Escuela de Kinesiología, Facultad de Salud y Odontología, Universidad Diego Portales, Santiago, Chile
josecarrasco@ug.uchile.cl, mauricio.cerda@uchile.cl

Abstract. State of the art in the area of image processing and machine learning shows significant advances in the estimation of human posture in 2D and 3D. However, it has not been accurately reported whether the use of these methodologies provides per joint plane of motion information within the range of error of clinical measurements (5°).

The purpose of this work was to select a method for estimating human posture in 3D with a monocular camera from the state of the art and to statistically compare it with clinical measurements in the angular variables.

A discriminative method for estimating human posture was trained with the Human3.6M database, and results were obtained from the performance of the posture estimation model in 3D with a monocular camera. Subsequently, angular variables were obtained by plane of movement per predicted joint.

Our results show that are joints with less than 5° of error in a plane of movements, such as the knee and elbow in the sagittal plane and the wrist in the frontal plane. On the other hand, in other joints such as the hip and ankle, its results are dependent on the action, the time periods of the evaluated actions, and the view of the camera.

Keywords: Human pose estimation · Physical examination · Biomechanics

1 Introduction

Human movement can be described through kinematics, and joint movement depends on the degrees of freedom of the types of synovial joints, which require a description in three dimensions or in each plane of movement [1]. The planes of movement are described based on the anatomical position of a standing person. The sagittal plane is parallel to the

Supplementary Information The online version contains supplementary material available at https://doi.org/10.1007/978-3-030-98457-1_10.

skull suture, dividing the body into the right and left sides. The frontal plane is parallel to the coronal suture of the skull, dividing the body into anterior and posterior. And the transverse plane is parallel to the horizontal and divides the body into an upper and a lower part [2]. Each joint has a bone that rotates with an axis perpendicular to the plane of motion. The planes of movement and axes allow establishing a system of convention, which is used in a relative way. This means that the position of a distal segment is relative to a proximal segment. For example, in the knee joint, the proximal segment that makes up the joint is the thigh, and the distal segment is the leg. Regardless of what position the other segments such as the spine, hip, or ankle are in, the description of joint movement by plane of movement allows us to understand the biomechanical behavior of the structures and the morphology of each joint. In a clinical evaluation, joint motion is measured by plane of motion and quantified in degrees [1].

1.1   Joint Movement Assessment in Clinical and Research Context

There are different tools and equipment to evaluate and quantify joint movement. The simplest is with the use of a goniometer. With goniometry, one can passively or actively assess the static angular position of the joint position. This is an evaluation by planes and not by a combination of planes of motion [3]. The error reported with goniometry measurements is classically 5° with high inter-and intra-rater reliability [3].

The electrogoniometers are used to obtain the range of motion in degrees dynamically [1, 3]. These have two arms, just like goniometers connected by a potentiometer. Electrogoniometers only generate a measurement in two planes of motion [3]. The error reported in the electrogoniometers literature is on average 3.5° [4].

The Gold Standard for the measurement of human movement that involves three dimensions, and all planes of joint movement is with an optical capture system with optoelectronic cameras with passive or active markers in anatomical landmarks and anthropometric measurement. These require a configuration of 6 to 10 optoelectronic cameras, a physical place to position them (there is a portable configuration) and require calibration of the cameras. The system captures the movement made by the person and calculates the 3D trajectories of the markers. Each marker must be visible by at least three cameras, and if there are occlusions of the markers in the direction of the camera's vision, by interpolation it can be obtained the position of the marker. And finally, it requires a software to interpolate and filter the raw data captured from the markers and generate a model or skeleton. All these software's and space requirements generate high costs to acquire this type of instrument. However, the error in the detection of the marker by the cameras is less than 1 mm, and there are reports that the mean square error in degrees is less than 1° in the detection of the angle, if the correct positioning of the markers is followed [5].

There are other options, such as the use of inertial sensors that capture movement based on sensors with accelerometer, gyroscope, and magnetometer. With these three sensors, the orientation of the segments is obtained in three dimensions, which allows obtaining kinematic information of the joints. These solve the occlusion of the markers in optical systems, since they are portable devices with a wireless connection with a data capture transmission radius in the order of 30 m, so it no longer depends on a limited volume of capture space. Noraxon, one of the manufacturers of inertial sensors, reported that the error in static positions is 0.4°, and in movements, the error is 1.2° [6].

1.2 Joint Movement Assessment Alternatives: Human Pose Estimation with Monocular Camera

Estimating human posture and movement from an image or a sequence of images (a video) is a process that requires computer vision techniques [7]. It is a topic of interest that has received attention, and each year there are more publications related to the estimation of human posture and movement in 3D [8]. In the last ten years, the number of related articles has approximately tripled from 385 to 1685 (using the keywords "3D human pose estimation", "3D motion tracking", "3D pose recovery", "3D motion tracking" in Science Direct comparing the period 2008–2020).

The reconstruction of the human posture in 3D in monocular images or in a sequence of images is a difficult task to carry out, due to the non-linear behavior of movement, the variability of shapes, clothes, difficult environments, and occlusions of a body segment by itself [7, 8].

Human pose estimation methods are classified according to how the body structure is interpreted. In literature, there are general method for estimate human posture: generative methods, discriminative methods, based on parts methods and hybrid methods [7, 8], being the discriminative methods the ones that have most captured the attention of researchers. The discriminative model or free model does not assume a particular model since it learns to map between images what is the position of the posture. Free models based on learning learn a function to map from the observations of an image to the posture in space and require a generalization concept in a test set [8].

Within the learning-based methods to estimate posture in 3D, the use of Deep Learning stands out [9–13] these require a database to train and test the estimate made. Most Deep Learning methods work on joint point regression and joint point detection. The input for both tasks is the bounding box images containing human subjects, and the goal of the regression task is to estimate the positions of the joint points in relation to the root or reference joint position (by convention, this is the pelvis). The goal of each detection task is to classify whether a local window contains a specific joint or not [10]. The advantage of this method is that it does not depend on delivering the characteristics as input [8].

The performance of 3D posture estimation methods with a monocular camera is described based on the average error per joint in millimeters, a Euclidean distance between the actual position and the predicted position of the center of the joint. The mean error per joint position of different types of posture estimators has been established [14]. The mean error ranges from 35.8 mm to 224.9 mm depending on the nature of the movement, and the database used to train and validate.

There are currently many published human pose estimation methods with a monocular camera. However, it has not been accurately reported whether the use of these methodologies provides information by plane of motion of the physical evaluation of joint position within the range of error of clinical measurements. In this research we propose a new metric to determine the performance of a 3D pose estimation with monocular camara, which is to calculate the average error of the estimation per plane of movement, since it has a direct clinical interpretation because the range of motion of a joint has a relationship with the human function. Also, it is important to determine this parameter so that it can be compared with other ways of measuring joint position.

2   Methods

2.1   Train a State-of-the-Art Posture Estimation Method with the Human 3.6M Database

The 3D posture estimation method with a monocular camera by Martinez [11] was used due to its results regarding the state of the art, easy implementation, and training time. It is a discriminative method based on learning with deep learning, the architecture used is in Fig. 1, which applies two completely connected layers with a residual connection of 2D to 3D regression key points.

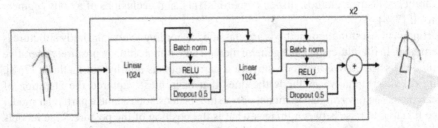

Fig. 1. The convolutional neural network proposed in Martínez's publication [11].

The model requires a training phase in its algorithm. To train the Human3.6M database was used [15].

The relative articular position in 3D requires anthropometric information of the people measured (length of a body segment). It is called relative since a root joint is defined, which is the pelvis, which is a reference to the coordinate system to estimate the position of the other joints. The kinematic representation considers the relative angles between segments. This makes it invariant to the scale and to the anthropometric characteristics of the body.

The database is publicly accessible and consists of 3.6 million images of different static postures or characteristic movements of human movement in 3 dimensions [15]. The database was developed with 11 professional actor subjects (6 men and 5 women), and 17 scenarios or actions were requested from the subjects. Each subject and action were recorded by 4 high-resolution calibrated cameras with a capture frequency of 50 Hz in a capture space 4 m wide and 3 m long on a flat surface. Simultaneously, the capture laboratory uses 10 infrared optoelectronic cameras, which allows it to capture the position of passive markers in anatomical landmarks of the subjects; the latter generates the position of each joint in 3D and the orientation of each body segment. The latter allows obtaining the kinematic representation of the movement of the subject of each joint. This database allows each image to have information on 3D joint position, segment orientation, and kinematic data [15].

For the use of the Human3.6M database, there is a standard protocol that uses subjects 1, 5, 6, 7, and 8 as part of the method training set. Subjects 9 and 11 are occupied as a test set [11].

The neural network training was carried out with 200 epochs using ADAM as a stochastic optimization method, with a learning rate of 0.001 with exponential decay and using a minibatch with a size of 64. The code was implemented in python and TensorFlow with a card Titan Xp GPU. NVIDIA® Quadro® 4000.

We use two variables to measure training performance. The mean per joint position error and the mean joint angle error.

One of the most used metrics is Mean Per Joint Position Error (MPJPE) [9] which is the Euclidean distance between the real position of the joint and the predicted position of each joint. N is the number of joints, T is the number of examples (number of images), $J_i^{(t)}$ is the position of the predicted joint, $J_i^{(root)}$ is the position of the predicted root joint (the pelvis), $J_i^{(t)}$ is the true position of the predicted joint $J_i^{(root)}$ is the true position of the root joint. This error is calculated with all the estimated joints, and they are added to obtain the average error (Eq. 1).

$$MPJPE = \frac{1}{T}\frac{1}{N} \sum_{t=1}^{T} \sum_{t=1}^{N} \|(J_i^{(t)} - J_{root}^{(t)}) - (j_i^{(t)} - j_{root}^{(t)})\|_2 \qquad (1)$$

There is another metric for evaluating joint angle error based on degrees. It is called the Mean Joint Angle Error (MJAE), which is the absolute average between the predicted angle and the actual angle in degrees based on the orientation of the body with respect to the camera. M is the number of joints, y_I is the estimated angle Y_i is the ground truth and mod is the modulus (Eq. 2) [16, 17].

$$MJAE = \frac{\sum_{i=I}^{M} |(y_I - Y_i) mod \pm 180°|}{M} \qquad (2)$$

2.2 Apply Clinical Context Metrics in the Human 3.6M Database

Subsequently, we propose a new metric to measure the average error of the angle per joint and per plane of movement (sagittal, frontal, and transverse planes) of the posture estimation methods with monocular camera. This variable is what allows us to compare with the variables of clinical measurements. The calculation of the angle of the joint depends on the position of the body segments that compose it and the observed plane. The joints considered are of the lower extremities, the ankle-foot, knee, and hip complex, of the upper extremities the wrist, elbow, and shoulder, and of the spine, the craniocervical region, and thoracolumbar are considered.

The Human 3.6M database contains the orientation of each body segment in a rotation matrix. With the orientation of the proximal and distal segments of the joint, each plane can be obtained.

To calculate the angle of each plane, the axis of rotation of the plane must be identified and the described angle calculated considering the reference as a vector, as shown in Fig. 2.

The relative angle of each joint by plane of movement was obtained (the rotation about the X, Y, and Z axes was used as a reference) through the inverse cosine function of the dot product of the vectors divided by the norm of the vectors (Eq. 3):

$$\theta = arcos\left(\frac{x \cdot y}{|x||y|}\right) \tag{3}$$

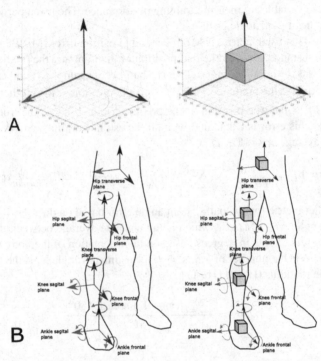

Fig. 2. A) Graphic representation of a reference system with unit vectors (left) and how this reference system provides the orientation of an object or segment (right). B) Relative segments orientation based on unit vectors, the orientation of each segment is obtained from a database rotation matrix.

Finally, the difference between the real angle and that predicted by the model in each sequence of images is obtained. In this way, we obtain the error of each joint in each plane of motion.

3   Results

3.1   Train a State-of-the-Art Posture Estimation Method with the Human 3.6M Database

In the training of the 3D human posture estimator, the loss function of the mean error of the position per joint of all the actions of the validation group was obtained, which can be observed in Fig. 3 the error obtained by epoch.

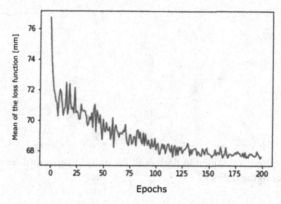

Fig. 3. Loss of training function graph of the neural network of Martínez's [11].

Results obtained in the model training range from 50.88 mm to 100.16 mm of error. The smallest error was obtained in the action of walking and the largest error was in the action of sitting down on the ground as show in Fig. 4.

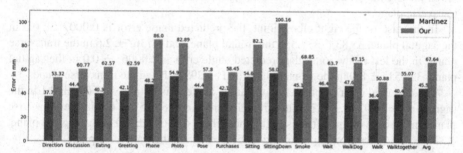

Fig. 4. Mean Per Joint Position Error in mm of the training published by Martinez (in blue) and the training performed (in orange) per action and its mean value. Difference in the results obtained from [11] and from the training carried out in this research from a range of 13.4 mm to 42.16 mm. (Color figure online)

The results of the average angular error per joint of the test subject prediction per action of the data set are in Fig. 5. The observed results of the average angular error per joint per action have a range of 12.04° to 35.98°. The action of walking is the one that presents the least error, and the action of sitting on the ground is the one that presents the greatest error.

3.2 Apply Clinical Context Metrics in the Human 3.6M Database

Table 1 presents the results of the error calculated by the plane of movement of each joint in degrees, the average, and the standard deviation. The details of the results by plane of movement in each action evaluated can be found in the supplementary material.

Figure 6 show error graphs grouped by plane of each joint. The error of each right and left joint of the upper and lower extremities and of the spine of the cervical area and

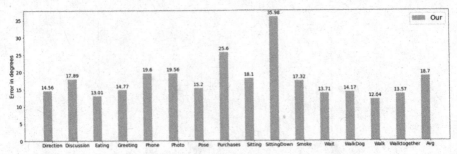

Fig. 5. Mean angular error per joint in degrees of the training performed (in orange) per action and its mean. (Color figure online)

the thoracolumbar area was calculated. Next, the joints that show an error of less than 5° on average in at least one plane of movement will be described.

It is observed that the error of the angle of the right knee joint is 0.0004° ± 0.0 in the sagittal plane, 33.095° ± 23.3 in the frontal plane, and 5.140° ± 2.0 in the transverse plane. In the left knee joint, it is obtained that the prediction has an error of 0.0004° ± 0.0 in the sagittal plane, 32.303° ± 24.0 in the frontal plane, and 8.982° ± 1.4 in the transverse plane.

In the case of the right elbow joint, the predicted angle error is 0.0007° ± 0.0 in the sagittal plane, 35.833° ± 7.5 in the frontal plane, and 6.736° ± 2.6 in the transverse plane. In the left elbow joint, the predicted angle error is 0.0006° ± 0.0 in the sagittal plane, 32.251° ± 8.0 in the frontal plane, and 5.429° ± 1.5 in the transverse plane.

The observed error of predicting the angle at the wrist joint is 70.669° ± 8.1 in the sagittal plane, 1.924° ± 0.7 in the frontal plane, and 16.625° ± 6.7 in the transverse plane. In the case of the left wrist joint, the error is 67.367° ± 7.0 in the sagittal plane, 1.320° ± 0.8 in the frontal plane, and 20.510° ± 8.8 in the transverse plane.

Table 1. Summary of results of the angular error in degree in each plane of movement per joint. Mean ± standard deviation. S: Sagital; F: Frontal; T: Transversal; Shou: Shoulder.

Plane	R. Hip	L. Hip	R. Knee	L. Knee	R. Ankle	L. Ankle	R. Shou
S	15.7 ± 3.8	12.7 ± 3.5	0.0004 ± 0	0.00004 ± 0	9.5 ± 3	5.6 ± 2.2	16.6 ± 3.8
F	17.1 ± 11.2	18.1 ± 10	33.1 ± 23.3	32.3 ± 24.0	7.9 ± 1.8	5.8 ± 2.4	19.5 ± 8.3
T	26.6 ± 8.7	23.9 ± 8.2	5.2 ± 2	8.9 ± 1.4	66.3 ± 5.9	67.9 ± 4.7	35.1 ± 11.4
Plane	L. Shou	R. Elbow	L. Elbow	R. Wrist	L. Wrist	Cervical	Lumbar
S	15.5 ± 5.5	0.0007 ± 0	0.0006 ± 0	70.7 ± 8.1	67.4 ± 7.0	8.2 ± 3.0	12.1 ± 9.3
F	21.5 ± 8.8	35.8 ± 7.5	32.3 ± 8.0	1.9 ± 0.7	1.3 ± 0.8	40.9 ± 9.8	16.0 ± 12
T	32.4 ± 8.1	6.7 ± 2.6	5.4 ± 1.5	16.6 ± 6.7	20.5 ± 8.8	47.7 ± 12.6	16.2 ± 4.3

The joints of the hip, ankle, shoulder, the craniocervical area, and thoracolumbar presented errors on average over 5° in all planes of movement. There are joints that present an error of less than 5° depending on the action evaluated (Supplementary material Tables 1–9).

The joints that present an error of less than 5° in certain actions in the sagittal plane are the ankle in the actions of direction, discussion, eating, greeting, photo, and walking (Table 1 in the supplementary material)—the cervical area in the discussion and eating actions (Table 3 in the supplementary material). The lumbar area in the actions of direction, posing, walking, and walking in company (Table 3 in the supplementary material).

The joints that present an error of less than 5° in certain actions in the frontal plane are the hip in the action of arguing (Table 4 in the supplementary material). The ankle in the actions of discussing, eating, greeting, talking on the phone, walking, and walking in company (Table 4 in the supplementary material). In the lumbar area in the action of greeting (Table 6 in the supplementary material).

The joints that present an error of less than 5° in certain actions in the frontal plane are the knee in the actions of discussing, greeting, talking on the phone, posing, shopping, walking with the dog, walking, and walking in company (Table 7 in the Supplementary material). The elbow in the actions of management, arguing, greeting, talking on the phone, posing, shopping, walking with the dog, and walking in company (Table 8 in the supplementary material).

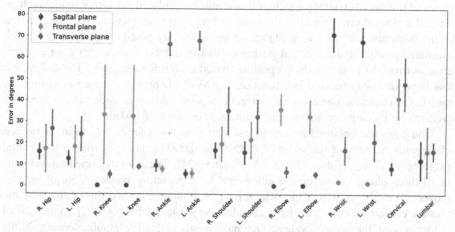

Fig. 6. Graph of the angular error by plane of movement of the right and left lower extremities, right and left upper extremities, cervical and lumbar spine. The point represents the mean error, and the bar represents the standard deviation.

4 Discussion

In the development of this work, a difference is observed between the results of the average error per joint per action and the average of the results obtained by Martinez [11] and those obtained by us, even replicating the parameters specified by the authors. An explanation for this result is the random assignment of weights and bias of the network, which produces different results of the training of the network, even replicating the parameters [18]. Interestingly, even in the face of this increase in error, we were able to obtain the measurement of the angles by joint planes with a fairly reliable prediction close to the real value in the knee joint, the elbow in the sagittal plane, and the wrist. In the frontal plane, as well as in certain actions, joints with an error under 5° such as the ankle, the cervical and thoracolumbar cranial zone in the sagittal plane, the hip, the ankle, and the thoracolumbar zone in the frontal plane and in the transversal plane joints of the knee and elbow. As described [14, 19], a low average error of the position of the joint does not always indicate that the estimation of posture is more accurate. This is because the estimate depends on the human shape, scale, and skeleton. This is still an open problem and is under discussion in this methodology. The latter may explain the reason for obtaining high errors in the position of the joint and still obtaining low errors in the calculation of the angle per plane.

The result of the average angular error of the joint per action is a metric that was not calculated with the Martinez posture estimation method [14]. Measuring training performance through the above does not allow obtaining sufficient information for a clinical evaluator who requires movement planes to establish the measurement error with a 3D posture estimator with a monocular camera. The average error of the joint position is one of the most used metrics. However, there are other suggested metrics to measure the loss of training function that could be explored for future work, such as the reconstructed error, which is the same average error calculation, from the position of the posterior joint to a rigid alignment performed by post-processing between the estimated posture and the actual position. Another metric is the mean joint position error normalized to the predicted position based on a reference scale. The last metric that is beginning to be used as a function of loss of 3D posture estimation methods is the 3D version of the percentage of correct key points, which considers that a joint was predicted in its correct position with a threshold distance of 150 mm. [14].

The joints that obtained an error of less than 5° are the knee and elbow in the sagittal plane with an error of the order of 0.0004° to 0.0007°, and the wrist in the frontal plane with an error of the order of 1.320°. At 1.924°. These joints present movements in all three planes; however, the elbow and knee present a greater range of angular movement in the sagittal plane, which may be fundamental and the reason why the training carried out finds it easier to calculate the angles in this plane [2]. In the case of the wrist joint, the actions evaluated are movements with a low amplitude range of the frontal plane. This may be a reason for the low estimation error. The wrist has flexion-extension movements that are naturally accompanied by osteokinematic movements of low amplitude radialization and ulnarization by the well-known dart thrower pattern. This movement of radialization and ulnarization can increase in cases of using the hands in the movement of objects with weight [20]. As it was observed in this work, there are joints of the human body that the angle cannot be predicted, or the prediction error is severely high. This is consistent with findings of the difficulty of predicting the position of the joint in the foot – ankle, hand-wrist area, and the cervical area [11].

Articulation error per plane of motion may increase or decrease based on the nature or characteristics of the motion. The three main variables that were observed that generate changes are: if the movement carried out by the person entails a displacement within the capture space, if the posture or the observed joint is in a static position, and finally, the occlusions of the segments. This should generate a change in the methodology of estimating the performance of 3D posture estimation methods with a monocular camera, from the generation of databases to training these models and the reported results to be able to distinguish and select a posture estimation method based on the nature of the movements according to the joint that needs to be studied or evaluated. In the work of [11], they conclude that the error in certain joints in actions such as taking photos, talking on the phone, sitting, and sitting on the floor is due to severe auto-occlusion, which prevent observing the hand or the lower extremities are aligned with the trunk [11]. This can change depending on the dataset used for training. In this case, human 3.6M does not have to deal woth changing lights because they are recording indoor human motion. In the case of using a dataset in the wild, this can be a factor to consider in the increase of the error. For the purpose of assessing movement in a clinical context, the measurement of the human motion can be confined to a closed environment.

To make posture in 3D with a neural network with a monocular camera an alternative to clinical measurement: movements should be isolated or specific, evaluated subject does not perform displacement or avoid displacement in the capture zone, and to request movements that do not involve rotation about its own axis and avoid occlusions of its segments. The movements that we recommend evaluating with this method are: (i) Reaching with the upper limb without interaction with objects, since the database with which the prediction model was trained does not involve occlusions of people with objects. (ii) Maintained postures of the upper extremities, lower extremities, and spine at different ranges of motion. (iii) The evaluation of a repetitive movement that involves the elbow, wrist, and knee joints and evaluating if it meets a certain range to consider a count of a movement as is the case of exercises without interaction with objects (squats, lunges and planks).

Considering our results, it is suggested that when evaluating with these measurements, the quality of a movement (variables such as speed and its derivatives) with this method of estimating posture in 3D with a monocular camera, filters for the variability are used for the variability and dispersion that you can obtain in each frame of the video. If there is wide variability in joints, a measurement of the angular velocity would be overestimated by its noise.

Every year, new methods of posture estimators in 3D with a monocular camera are published [8]; [14], which presents a lower error. We suggest, based on the results of this research, that they should be evaluated based on this methodology by plane of movement. As there are no works evaluating these or similar metrics, we cannot make a prediction if this can be used as a reliable method of studying human movement by plane in 3D. The 3D posture estimation methods that we can consider should involve those who perform model training with neural networks as well as generative and hybrid methods since the literature has not ruled out the performance of these models. The possibility of adding this metric to the performance measurement of 3D posture estimators with a monocular camera will allow us to take the next step to complement its application in the field of health, physical rehabilitation, and sports [21]. Even future work could consider that the loss function is based on orientations and not positions of the joints.

Several studies have concluded that a successful application of 3D posture estimators with monocular and multicamera cameras should be able to obtain these results in closed and open places, where lighting, background conditions, and human behavior are not controlled. However, such methods are trained specifically for certain conditions, such as Human3.6. Thus, more research should be carried on the robustness under such conditions [8].

5   Conclusion

Retrieving or measuring human movement through the estimation of human posture from RGB images or videos has attracted the attention of multiple research groups. This is due to not requiring sensors that must be positioned in the segments and its applicability in different areas such as the human-computer interface, robotics, video analysis, and augmented reality. There are extensive works on this area of 2D and 3D monocular camera posture estimation, but few studies evaluate its clinical use, and these use joint position and relative angle without obtaining the angle per plane of motion of each joint involved. It is the angle per plane of motion that is of greatest clinical interest.

This research work allowed us to explore a new metric to test the performance of a posture estimator with a 3D monocular camera which seeks the orientation of the segments, and to use a measurement that can be extrapolated into a clinical language for the physical evaluation of human movement. This metric was used to evaluate Martinez's monocular camera 3D posture estimation method [11], concluding that it is possible to use it to predict the movement of the elbow and wrist, which are used for reaching or manipulating tasks; and in the case of the knee to analyze tasks that involve movements such as walking or transitions in a closed kinematic chain such as the transition from sitting to standing (sitting bipedal transition). More specifically, we were able to verify that in order to reduce the error in the prediction of the joint position in the three planes of movement, the occlusions of the person's segments should be avoided, prioritizing actions of static postures and, if the patient performs displacement, avoid turning on their own axis.

Future work should be oriented to test methods of posture estimation in 3D to determine its use as an alternative to quantifying joint measurement, determining its performance to obtain fewer errors in each joint per plane of movement. Also, observe and study these methods as an opportunity for feedback for exercises, especially in a historical moment where physical rehabilitation has had to abruptly transform from a face-to-face format to telerehabilitation.

In addition, in light of the results, it should be considered that the development of the following databases for the estimation of human posture in 2D and 3D should be composed of functional movements related to activities of daily life such as dressing, displacement, going up or downstairs, running, movements with different natures of the open or closed kinetic chain, human-object interaction, weight-bearing or interaction with objects to bring the evaluation closer to the function of the person not only in a clinical context, opening the possibility of using these methods in ergonomic evaluations.

Acknowledgments. The authors acknowledge the support of Agencia Nacional de Investigación y Desarrollo (ANID) grants FONDECYT 1221696, FONDEQUIP EQM210020, as well as PIA Anillo ACT192015.

References

1. Winter, D.A.: Biomechanics and Motor Control of Human Movement (2009). https://doi.org/10.1002/9780470549148
2. Neumann, D.A.: Kinesiology of the Musculoskeletal System: Foundations for Rehabilitation. Mosby (2010)
3. Norkin, C.C., Joyce White, D.: Measurement of Joint Motion: A Guide to Goniometry. F.A. Davis (2016)
4. Piriyaprasarth, P., Morris, M.E.: Psychometric properties of measurement tools for quantifying knee joint position and movement: a systematic review. Knee **14**(1), 2–8 (2007)
5. Chèze, L.: Kinematic Analysis of Human Movement (2014). https://doi.org/10.1002/9781119058144
6. Seidel, D.H., D'Souza, S.F., Alt, W.W., Wachowsky, M.: Comparison of an inertial sensor based motion measurement system with a 3D-reflex marker based motion capture system. Gait Posture **42**, S75 (2015)
7. Moeslund, T.B., Hilton, A., Krüger, V., Sigal, L.: Visual Analysis of Humans: Looking at People. Springer, Heidelberg (2011). https://doi.org/10.1007/978-0-85729-997-0
8. Sarafianos, N., Boteanu, B., Ionescu, B., Kakadiaris, I.A.: 3D Human pose estimation: a review of the literature and analysis of covariates. Comput. Vis. Image Underst. **152**, 1–20 (2016). https://doi.org/10.1016/j.cviu.2016.09.002
9. Chen, C.-H., Ramanan, D.: 3D human pose estimation = 2D pose estimation matching. In: 2017 IEEE Conference on Computer Vision and Pattern Recognition (CVPR) (2017). https://doi.org/10.1109/cvpr.2017.610
10. Li, S., Chan, A.B.: 3D human pose estimation from monocular images with deep convolutional neural network. In: Cremers, D., Reid, I., Saito, H., Yang, M.-H. (eds.) ACCV 2014. LNCS, vol. 9004, pp. 332–347. Springer, Cham (2015). https://doi.org/10.1007/978-3-319-16808-1_23
11. Martinez, J., Hossain, R., Romero, J., Little, J.J.: A simple yet effective baseline for 3D human pose estimation. In: 2017 IEEE International Conference on Computer Vision (ICCV) (2017). https://doi.org/10.1109/iccv.2017.288
12. Sun, X., Xiao, B., Wei, F., Liang, S., Wei, Y.: Integral human pose regression. In: Ferrari, V., Hebert, M., Sminchisescu, C., Weiss, Y. (eds.) ECCV 2018. LNCS, vol. 11210, pp. 536–553. Springer, Cham (2018). https://doi.org/10.1007/978-3-030-01231-1_33
13. Zhou, X., Huang, Q., Sun, X., Xue, X., Wei, Y.: Towards 3D human pose estimation in the wild: a weakly-supervised approach. In: 2017 IEEE International Conference on Computer Vision (ICCV) (2017). https://doi.org/10.1109/iccv.2017.51
14. Ji, X., Fang, Q., Dong, J., Shuai, Q., Jiang, W., Zhou, X.: A survey on monocular 3D human pose estimation. Virtual Reality Intell. Hardw. **2**(6), 471–500 (2020). https://doi.org/10.1016/j.vrih.2020.04.005
15. Ionescu, C., Papava, D., Olaru, V., Sminchisescu, C.: Human3.6M: large scale datasets and predictive methods for 3D human sensing in natural environments. IEEE Trans. Pattern Anal. Mach. Intell. **36**(7), 1325–1339 (2014). https://doi.org/10.1109/TPAMI.2013.248
16. Agarwal, A., Triggs, B.: Recovering 3D human pose from monocular images. IEEE Trans. Pattern Anal. Mach. Intell. **28**(1), 44–58 (2006)
17. Ning, H., Xu, W., Gong, Y., Huang, T.: Discriminative learning of visual words for 3D human pose estimation. In: 2008 IEEE Conference on Computer Vision and Pattern Recognition (2008). https://doi.org/10.1109/cvpr.2008.4587534
18. Kinsley, H., Kukieła, D.: Neural networks from scratch in Python (2020)
19. Dang, Q., Yin, J., Wang, B., Zheng, W.: Deep learning based 2D human pose estimation: a survey. Tsinghua Sci. Technol. **24**(6), 663–676 (2019). https://doi.org/10.26599/TST.2018.9010100

20. Brigstocke, G.H.O., Hearnden, A., Holt, C., Whatling, G.: In-vivo confirmation of the use of the dart thrower's motion during activities of daily living. J. Hand Surg.: Eur. **39**(4), 373–378 (2014). https://doi.org/10.1177/1753193412460149
21. Prima, O.D.A., Imabuchi, T.: Single camera 3D human pose estimation for tele-rehabilitation. In: ETelemed 2019, pp. 13–18 (2019)

On the Performance of Preconditioned Methods to Solve L^p-Norm Phase Unwrapping

Ricardo Legarda-Saenz$^{(\boxtimes)}$ ⓘ, Carlos Brito-Loeza ⓘ,
and Arturo Espinosa-Romero ⓘ

CLIR at Facultad de Matematicas, Universidad Autonoma de Yucatan,
Mérida, Mexico
{rlegarda,carlos.brito}@correo.uady.mx
http://clir-lab.org

Abstract. In this paper, we analyze and evaluate suitable preconditioning techniques to improve the performance of the L^p-norm phase unwrapping method. We consider five preconditioning techniques commonly found in the literature, and analyze their performance with different sizes of wrapped-phase maps.

Keywords: Phase unwrapping · L^p-norm based method · Preconditioning techniques

1 Introduction

There has been a growing interest in the development of new techniques for the processing of coherent signals. This kind of signals is generated by measurement techniques like synthetic aperture radar (SAR), magnetic resonance imaging (MRI), and interferometry among others. The objective of this processing is to estimate the phase term $\phi_\mathbf{x}$, also known as phase map, from a signal which general model could be expressed as

$$U_\mathbf{x} = S_\mathbf{x} \exp\left(i\phi_\mathbf{x}\right),$$

where $\mathbf{x} = (x, y)$ is the position and $S_\mathbf{x}$ is the signal amplitude. The estimation of the phase term $\phi_\mathbf{x}$ becomes very relevant, given that this term can be related to different physical quantities such as geographical topography in the case of SAR, or the optical path difference in the case of optical interferometry [6,19].

However, as it can be seen from the signal model, the estimation of the phase term $\phi_\mathbf{x}$ is not straightforward. Instead, the estimated phase map from the signal is defined as

$$\psi_\mathbf{x} = \phi_\mathbf{x} + 2\pi k_\mathbf{x}, \tag{1}$$

where $k_\mathbf{x}$ is a function that bounds the values to $-\pi < \psi_\mathbf{x} \le \pi$. The term $\psi_\mathbf{x}$ is known as wrapped phase and is a nonlinear function of $\phi_\mathbf{x}$. This term is not

© Springer Nature Switzerland AG 2022
C. Brito-Loeza et al. (Eds.): ISICS 2022, CCIS 1569, pp. 135–144, 2022.
https://doi.org/10.1007/978-3-030-98457-1_11

useful for measurements because just offers the principal values of the phase term $\phi_\mathbf{x}$, so it is necessary estimate $\phi_\mathbf{x}$ from this wrapped phase $\psi_\mathbf{x}$. This process is called phase unwrapping [8].

Phase unwrapping is an ill-posed problem [1,20]. The unwrapping process consists of integrating the gradient field of the wrapped phase map [8]. Even in ideal conditions, phase estimation is not trivial due to the non linearity of $\psi_\mathbf{x}$ caused by cyclic discontinuities. In real conditions, the unwrapping process becomes very difficult, where noise signal, sub-sampling or differences larger than 2π (real or not) generate ambiguities hard to process not allowing the accurate recovering of the phase map $\phi_\mathbf{x}$.

In the literature there are two main strategies to solve the unwrapping problem [7,8]: the first one, known as path-following or local methods, consists of integrating the differences of the wrapped phase over a path that covers the entire phase map. The second one, considers the problem globally and the solution is presented in the form of an integral over the wrapped region. In the global strategy, there are two approaches: the first consists of using Green functions together with a numerical solution based on the Fourier transform [4,5,13,14].

The second approach expresses the solution as a L^p-norm minimization problem, resulting on the solution of weighted differential equations. The numerical solution of these differential equations leads to a nonlinear system $\mathbf{A}(\mathbf{u})\mathbf{u} = \mathbf{b}$, which has to be solved iteratively with great computational cost [9,11,12]. Typically, conjugate gradient (CG) or multigrid method are the methods of choice for this kind of problems. In the case of the conjugate gradient, matrix $\mathbf{A}$ is expected to be well conditioned, otherwise the convergence will be slow. However, very often one comes across with ill conditioned matrices when working with these nonlinear systems. The solution is to precondition the matrix $\mathbf{A}$; this is, instead of solving the original system $\mathbf{A}(\mathbf{u})\mathbf{u} = \mathbf{b}$, we solve the preconditioned system $\mathbf{M}^{-1}\mathbf{A}(\mathbf{u})\mathbf{u} = \mathbf{M}^{-1}\mathbf{b}$. The matrix $\mathbf{M}$, called a preconditioner for the matrix $\mathbf{A}$, is chosen to improve the condition number of the matrix $\mathbf{A}$. In most cases, this preconditioning matrix is problem dependent.

The goal of this paper is to analyze and evaluate suitable preconditioning techniques to improve the performance of the L^p-norm phase unwrapping method [8,9]. We consider five preconditioning techniques commonly found in the literature, and analyze their performance with different sizes of wrapped-phase maps. The organization of this paper is as follows: first, we describe the L^p-norm phase unwrapping method and their numerical solution. Then, the performance of the selected preconditioning techniques is evaluated by numerical experiments with different sizes of a synthetic wrapped-phase map. Finally, we discuss our results and present some concluding remarks.

2   Methodology

The L^p-norm based method proposed by D. C. Ghiglia and M.D. Pritt for 2-D phase unwrapping is defined as [9]

$$\min_{\phi} J(\phi_{\mathbf{x}}) = \iint_{\Omega} \left| \frac{\partial \phi}{\partial x} - \frac{\partial \psi}{\partial x} \right|^p + \left| \frac{\partial \phi}{\partial y} - \frac{\partial \psi}{\partial y} \right|^p d\mathbf{x} \tag{2}$$

where $\mathbf{x} = (x, y)$, and $\Omega \subseteq \mathbb{R}^2$ is the domain of integration. To obtain the solution of the problem expressed in Eq. (2), the first-order optimality condition or Euler-Lagrange equation has to be derived, resulting in the following partial differential equation (PDE)

$$-\frac{\partial}{\partial x} \left[\left(\frac{\partial \phi}{\partial x} - \frac{\partial \psi}{\partial x} \right) \left| \frac{\partial \phi}{\partial x} - \frac{\partial \psi}{\partial x} \right|^{p-2} \right] - \frac{\partial}{\partial y} \left[\left(\frac{\partial \phi}{\partial y} - \frac{\partial \psi}{\partial y} \right) \left| \frac{\partial \phi}{\partial y} - \frac{\partial \psi}{\partial y} \right|^{p-2} \right] = 0,$$
$$\tag{3}$$

with boundary conditions

$$\left[\left(\frac{\partial \phi}{\partial x} - \frac{\partial \psi}{\partial x} \right) \left| \frac{\partial \phi}{\partial x} - \frac{\partial \psi}{\partial x} \right|^{p-2}, \ \left(\frac{\partial \phi}{\partial y} - \frac{\partial \psi}{\partial y} \right) \left| \frac{\partial \phi}{\partial y} - \frac{\partial \psi}{\partial y} \right|^{p-2} \right] \cdot \hat{\mathbf{n}} = 0,$$

where $\hat{\mathbf{n}}$ denotes the unit outer normal vector to the boundary.

2.1 Numerical solution

Let $u_{i,j} = u(x_i, y_j)$ to denote the value of a function $u_{\mathbf{x}}$ at point (x_i, y_j) defined on $\Omega = [a, b] \times [c, d]$, where the sampling points are $x_i = a + (i - 1)h_x$, $y_j = c + (j - 1)h_y$, with $1 \leq i \leq M$, $1 \leq j \leq N$, $h_x = (b - a)/(M - 1)$, $h_y = (d - c)/(N - 1)$ and M, N are the number of points in the discrete grid of points. We use u to represent any of the variables ϕ and ψ defined in the previous equations. Derivatives are approximated using standard forward and backward finite difference schemes

$$\delta_x^{\pm} u_{i,j} = \pm \frac{u_{i,j\pm1} - u_{i,j}}{h_x} \quad \text{and} \quad \delta_y^{\pm} u_{i,j} = \pm \frac{u_{i\pm1j} - u_{i,j}}{h_y}.$$

The gradient and the divergence are approximated as

$$\nabla u_{i,j} = (\delta_x^+ u_{i,j}, \delta_y^+ u_{i,j}) \quad \text{and} \quad \nabla \cdot \nabla u_{i,j} = \delta_x^-(\delta_x^+ u_{i,j}) + \delta_y^-(\delta_y^+ u_{i,j}),$$

respectively.

Hence the numerical approximation of the Eq. (3) is given by

$$-\delta_x^- \left[(\delta_x^+ \phi - \Delta_{i,j}^x) \left| \delta_x^+ \phi - \Delta_{i,j}^x \right|^{p-2} \right] - \delta_y^- \left[(\delta_y^+ \phi - \Delta_{i,j}^y) \left| \delta_y^+ \phi - \Delta_{i,j}^y \right|^{p-2} \right] = 0,$$
$$\tag{4}$$

with boundary conditions

$$\left[(\delta_x^+ \phi - \Delta_{i,j}^x) \left| \delta_x^+ \phi - \Delta_{i,j}^x \right|^{p-2}, \ (\delta_y^+ \phi - \Delta_{i,j}^y) \left| \delta_y^+ \phi - \Delta_{i,j}^y \right|^{p-2} \right] \cdot \hat{\mathbf{n}} = 0,$$

where the terms $\Delta_{i,j}^x$ y $\Delta_{i,j}^y$ are defined as

$$\Delta_{i,j}^x = \begin{cases} \mathcal{W}(\psi_{i,j+1} - \psi_{i,j}) & \text{if } 1 \leq i \leq M - 1, \ 1 \leq j \leq N - 2 \\ \mathcal{W}(\psi_{i,j} - \psi_{i,j-1}) & \text{if } 1 \leq i \leq M - 1, \ j = N - 1 \end{cases}$$

$$\Delta_{i,j}^y = \begin{cases} \mathcal{W}\left(\psi_{i+1,j} - \psi_{i,j}\right) & \text{if} \quad 1 \le i \le M-2,\, 1 \le j \le N-1 \\ \mathcal{W}\left(\psi_{i,j} - \psi_{i-1,j}\right) & \text{if} \quad i = M-1,\, 1 \le j \le N-1 \end{cases}$$

where $\mathcal{W}$ is the wrapping operator [8]. Applying the previous discrete approximations, we have that the numerical solution of Eq. (3) is given by

$$\begin{aligned} &\left(\phi_{i,j} - \phi_{i,j-1} - \Delta_{i,j-1}^x\right) U_{i,j-1} - \left(\phi_{i,j+1} - \phi_{i,j} - \Delta_{i,j}^x\right) U_{i,j} \\ &+ \left(\phi_{i,j} - \phi_{i-1,j} - \Delta_{i-1,j}^y\right) V_{i-1,j} - \left(\phi_{i+1,j} - \phi_{i,j} - \Delta_{i,j}^y\right) V_{i,j} = 0, \end{aligned} \tag{5}$$

with boundary conditions

$$\left[\left(\phi_{i,j+1} - \phi_{i,j} - \Delta_{i,j}^x\right) U_{i,j},\, \left(\phi_{i+1,j} - \phi_{i,j} - \Delta_{i,j}^y\right) V_{i,j}\right] \cdot \hat{\mathbf{n}} = 0,$$

where for simplicity and without loss of generality we consider $h_x = h_y = 1$. The terms U y V are defined as

$$U_{i,j} = \left|\phi_{i,j+1} - \phi_{i,j} - \Delta_{i,j}^x\right|^{p-2} = \frac{\tau}{\left|\phi_{i,j+1} - \phi_{i,j} - \Delta_{i,j}^x\right|^{2-p} + \tau},$$

$$V_{i,j} = \left|\phi_{i+1,j} - \phi_{i,j} - \Delta_{i,j}^y\right|^{p-2} = \frac{\tau}{\left|\phi_{i+1,j} - \phi_{i,j} - \Delta_{i,j}^y\right|^{2-p} + \tau}. \tag{6}$$

to force the values of the terms to lie in the range $(0, 1)$. This helps the stability and convergence of the numerical solution [2,9]. Usually, $\tau = 0.01$ is selected for phase unwrapping process [8,9].

Discretization of Eq. (3) leads to a nonlinear PDE because the terms U and V are functions of the input data and the solution. This is solved using the following iterative procedure [2,9,17]: first, given an initial value ϕ, the terms U and V are computed; then, the terms U and V are held fixed and Eq. (5) is solved using preconditioned conjugate gradient [10,18]. With the current solution ϕ, the terms U and V are updated and a new solution is computed. This process is repeated until convergence.

Now, we present the algorithm to solve the discretization of Eq. (3). First we arrange Eq. (5) in matrix form $\mathbf{A}\phi = \mathbf{b}$ as

$$\begin{aligned} &-\left(\phi_{i,j+1} U_{i,j} + \phi_{i+1,j} V_{i,j} + \phi_{i,j-1} U_{i,j-1} + \phi_{i-1,j} V_{i-1,j}\right) \\ &+ \left(U_{i,j-1} + U_{i,j} + V_{i-1,j} + V_{i,j}\right) \phi_{i,j} \\ &= \Delta_{i,j-1}^x U_{i,j-1} - \Delta_{i,j}^x U_{i,j} + \Delta_{i-1,j}^y V_{i-1,j} - \Delta_{i,j}^y V_{i,j}. \end{aligned} \tag{7}$$

Notice that $\mathbf{A}$ is a $MN \times MN$ sparse matrix which depends on the terms U and V, so it needs to be constructed at each iteration. The preconditioned conjugate gradient (PCG) used in our work is the implementation proposed in Ref. [18], and the explicit structure of the algorithm is given in Algorithm 1.

The key point of the performance of the algorithm is the proper selection of the preconditioning matrix $\mathbf{M}$, step 8 of Algorithm 1. $\mathbf{M}$ can be defined in many different ways but it should meet the following requirements: a) the preconditioned system should be easy to solve, and b) the preconditioning matrix should be computationally cheap to construct and apply [16].

Algorithm 1: L^p-norm phase unwrapping algorithm.

Data: the wrapped phase ψ and $p < 2$.

Result: the unwrapped phase ϕ.

```
 1  k ← 0, error ← 1
 2  φ^k_{i,j} ← random values
 3  while k < k_max and error > tol do
 4  │   compute U and V, Eq. (6)
 5  │   solve Eq. (7) using PCG:
 6  │   begin
 7  │   │   construct A and b
 8  │   │   estimate preconditioning matrix M from A
 9  │   │   φ^{k+1} ← φ^k
10  │   │   l ← 0
11  │   │   r ← b − Aφ^{k+1}
12  │   │   d ← M^{-1}r
13  │   │   δ_new ← r^T d
14  │   │   δ_0 ← δ_new
15  │   │   while l < l_max and δ_new > ε²δ_0 do
16  │   │   │   q ← Ad
17  │   │   │   α ← δ_new/d^T q
18  │   │   │   φ^{k+1} ← φ^{k+1} + αd
19  │   │   │   if l is divisible by √MN then
20  │   │   │   │   r ← b − Aφ^{k+1}
21  │   │   │   else
22  │   │   │   │   r ← r − αq
23  │   │   │   end
24  │   │   │   s ← M^{-1}r
25  │   │   │   δ_old ← δ_new
26  │   │   │   δ_new ← r^T s
27  │   │   │   β ← δ_new/δ_old
28  │   │   │   d ← s + βd
29  │   │   │   l ← l + 1
30  │   │   end
31  │   end
32  │   error ← ‖φ^{k+1}_{i,j} − φ^k_{i,j}‖/‖φ^k_{i,j}‖
33  │   k ← k + 1
34  end
```

Here we test suitable preconditioning techniques to estimate matrix $\mathbf{M}$ in Algorithm 1 and analyze the performance of the L^p-norm phase unwrapping method. For this purpose, we selected the following commonly found preconditioning techniques in literature [3,16,21]:

1. $\mathbf{M} \Leftarrow \mathbf{I}$, where $\mathbf{I}$ is the identity matrix; with this matrix, PCG becomes CG [10].

2. $\mathbf{M} \Leftarrow \mathbf{D}$, where $\mathbf{D}$ is the diagonal of matrix $\mathbf{A}$; this technique is known as Jacobi preconditioning.
3. $\mathbf{M} \Leftarrow ILU(\mathbf{A})$, the incomplete LU factorization with no fill-in.
4. $\mathbf{M} \Leftarrow IC(\mathbf{A})$, the incomplete Cholesky factorization with no fill-in.
5. $\mathbf{M} \Leftarrow SOR(\mathbf{A})$, the successive over-relaxation factorization.

The main reason for selecting these preconditioning techniques was their no fill-in property. That is, the preconditioning matrices preserve the sparse structure of matrix $\mathbf{A}$ and require just the same memory space used by matrix $\mathbf{A}$.

3   Numerical Experiments

To illustrate the performance of the selected preconditioning techniques, we carried out the numerical experiments using a Intel® Core™ i7 @ 2.40 GHz laptop with Debian GNU/Linux 10 (buster) 64-bit and 16 GB of memory. For our experiments, we programmed all the functions using C language, GNU g++ 8.3 compiler and Intel® MKL 2019 library. It is important to highlight that all the functions were programmed from scratch and were programmed from the basic algorithms, without using modifications that improve their performance.

We use the wrapped phase map shown in Fig. 1 as the data term ψ of the Algorithm 1. This wrapped phase map has a resolution of 640×480 pixels, and this resolution was used as our reference scale.

Fig. 1. Wrapped phase map used in the experiments.

We generated several scaled wrapped phase map from the one shown in Fig. 1, and used them as data in Algorithm 1. The scaled image sizes and the resultant sizes of sparse matrix $\mathbf{A}$ in our experiments are shown in Table 1.

Table 1. Image sizes used in the experiments.

Scale	Image size	Matrix **A**	
		Variables	Density (%)
0.25	160 × 120	95440	0.0250
0.50	320 × 240	382880	0.0064
0.75	480 × 360	862320	0.0028
1.00	640 × 480	1533760	0.0016
1.25	800 × 600	2397200	0.0010
1.50	960 × 720	3452640	0.0007
1.75	1120 × 840	4700080	0.0005
2.00	1280 × 960	6139520	0.0004

For each scaled wrapped phase map, we tested the selected five preconditioning matrices. The stopping criteria used in Algorithm 1 were $k_{max} = 500$, $tol = 10^{-6}$, $l_{max} = 2MN$, $\epsilon = 0.005$. Figure 2 shows the iterations needed to obtain the solution for the different scaled wrapped phase maps, and Fig. 3 shows the computational time consumed for each preconditioning technique. It is worth the value to remark that the time taken to construct preconditioning matrix **M**: except for the incomplete Cholesky factorization, all the preconditioning techniques employed between 1% and 2% of the total processing time. However, the incomplete Cholesky factorization took more than 90%. This is why in Figs. 2 and 3, we only show the first four experiments with this technique.

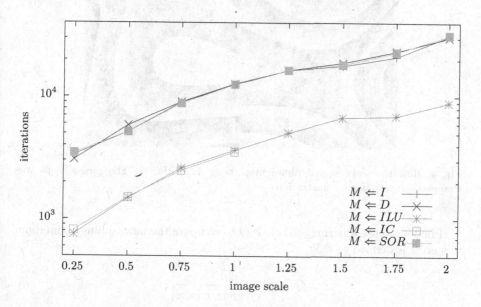

Fig. 2. Iterations employed for the different test.

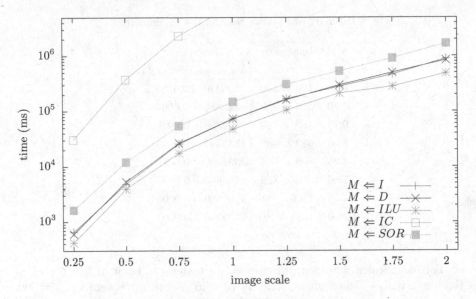

Fig. 3. Computational time used for the different test.

Fig. 4. Resultant unwrapped phase map using Algorithm 1. The phase maps was wrapped for purposes of illustration.

Finally, we use a normalized error Q to compare the unwrapping estimation; this error is defined as [15]:

$$Q(\mu, \nu) = \frac{\|\mu - \nu\|_2}{\|\mu\|_2 + \|\nu\|_2}, \tag{8}$$

where μ and ν are the signals to be compared. The normalized error values vary between zero (for perfect agreement) and one (for perfect disagreement). For all the cases, we found that the normalized error was around $Q = 0.17$. An example of the resultant unwrapped phase map is shown in Fig. 4.

4   Discussion of Results and Conclusions

From the results obtained, we have the following remarks. First, any of the techniques used had no impact on the obtained results, since for all the experiments the normalized error Q was approximately the same, $Q = 0.17$. The differences are evident when we analyze the performance in terms of iterations and computational time. If we only consider the number of iterations, the incomplete LU factorization and incomplete Cholesky factorization clearly show their advantage over the other three methods. However, this perception changes when we also consider the computational time used. Clearly, the incomplete Cholesky factorization consumed a lot of time which makes it unviable to be considered as a preconditioning technique. In general, numerical results show the incomplete LU factorization as the best choice to be used as preconditioning technique in Algorithm 1.

As work in the future, we are going to analyze the use of dedicated libraries for estimating the preconditioning matrix, where we hope to obtain better results.

References

1. Bertero, M., Boccacci, P.: Introduction to Inverse Problems in Imaging. Institute of Physics Publishing, Bristol (1998)
2. Bloomfield, P., Steiger, W.: Least Absolute Deviations: Theory, Applications and Algorithms. Birkhäuser, Boston (1983)
3. Chen, K.: Matrix Preconditioning Techniques and Applications. Cambridge University Press, Cambridge (2005)
4. Fornaro, G., Franceschetti, G., Lanari, R.: Interferometric SAR phase unwrapping using Green's formulation. IEEE Trans. Geosci. Remote Sens. **34**(3), 720–727 (1996). https://doi.org/10.1109/36.499751
5. Fornaro, G., Franceschetti, G., Lanari, R., Sansosti, E.: Robust phase-unwrapping techniques: a comparison. J. Opt. Soc. Am. A **13**(12), 2355–2366 (1996). https://doi.org/10.1364/JOSAA.13.002355
6. Gasvik, K.J.: Optical Metrology, 3rd edn. Wiley, Chichester (2002)
7. Gens, R.: Two-dimensional phase unwrapping for radar interferometry: developments and new challenges. Int. J. Remote Sens. **24**(4), 703–710 (2003). https://doi.org/10.1080/0143116021000016725
8. Ghiglia, D.C., Pritt, M.D.: Two-Dimensional Phase Unwrapping: Theory, Algorithms, and Software. Wiley-Interscience, New York (1998)
9. Ghiglia, D.C., Romero, L.A.: Minimum L p-norm two-dimensional phase unwrapping. J. Opt. Soc. Am. A **13**(10), 1999–2013 (1996). https://doi.org/10.1364/JOSAA.13.001999
10. Golub, G.H., Van Loan, C.F.: Matrix Computations, 3rd edn. Johns Hopkins University Press, Baltimore (1996)

11. Guo, Y., Chen, X., Zhang, T.: Robust phase unwrapping algorithm based on least squares. Opt. Lasers Eng. **63**, 25–29 (2014). https://doi.org/10.1016/j.optlaseng.2014.06.007
12. Hooper, A., Zebker, H.A.: Phase unwrapping in three dimensions with application to InSAR time series. J. Opt. Soc. Am. A **24**(9), 2737–2747 (2007). https://doi.org/10.1364/JOSAA.24.002737
13. Lyuboshenko, I.: Unwrapping circular interferograms. Appl. Opt. **39**(26), 4817–4825 (2000). https://doi.org/10.1364/AO.39.004817
14. Lyuboshenko, I., MaiTre, H.: Phase unwrapping for interferometric synthetic aperture radar by use of Helmholtz equation eigenfunctions and the first Green's identity. J. Opt. Soc. Am. A **16**(2), 378 (1999). https://doi.org/10.1364/JOSAA.16.000378
15. Perlin, M., Bustamante, M.D.: A robust quantitative comparison criterion of two signals based on the Sobolev norm of their difference. J. Eng. Math. **101**(1), 115–124 (2016). https://doi.org/10.1007/s10665-016-9849-7
16. Saad, Y.: Iterative Methods for Sparse Linear Systems, 2nd edn. SIAM (2003)
17. Scales, J.A., Gersztenkorn, A.: Robust methods in inverse theory. Inverse Probl. **4**(4), 1071–1091 (1988). https://doi.org/10.1088/0266-5611/4/4/010
18. Shewchuk, J.R.: An introduction to the conjugate gradient method without the agonizing pain. Technical report, Carnegie Mellon University, Pittsburgh (1994). https://www.cs.cmu.edu/~quake-papers/painless-conjugate-gradient.pdf
19. Tupin, F., Inglada, J., Nicolas, J.M.: Remote Sensing Imagery. Wiley-ISTE (2014)
20. Vogel, C.R.: Computational Methods for Inverse Problems. SIAM (2002)
21. van der Vorst, H.A.: Iterative Krylov Methods for Large Linear Systems. Cambridge University Press, Cambridge (2003)

Author Index

Printed in the United States
by Baker & Taylor Publisher Services